DIVOR

A practical consideration of all th
who feels their marriage has

By the same author
DEPRESSION
THE HEALING POWER OF HYPNOTISM
THE PREMENSTRUAL SYNDROME

DIVORCE
how to cope emotionally and practically

by

Caroline Shreeve
M.B., B.S.(Lond.), L.R.C.P., M.R.C.S.

TURNSTONE PRESS LIMITED
Wellingborough, Northamptonshire

First published 1984

© CAROLINE MOZELLE SHREEVE 1984

This book is sold subject to the condition that it shall not, by way of trade or otherwise, be lent, re-sold, hired out, or otherwise circulated without the publisher's prior consent in any form of binding or cover other than that in which it is published and without a similar condition including this condition being imposed on the subsequent purchaser.

> British Library Cataloguing in Publication Data
>
> Shreeve, Caroline
>   Divorce
>   1. Divorce — England
>   306.8'9'0942   HQ846
>
>   ISBN 0-85500-202-6

Turnstone Press is part of the Thorsons Publishing Group

Printed and bound in Great Britain

CONTENTS

		Page
	Introduction	7
Chapter		
1.	Why Marriage?	8
2.	Why Divorce?	21
3.	Seeking Advice	43
4.	Reaching a Decision	52
5.	Admitting Mistakes and Making the Break	70
6.	Separation or Divorce?	78
7.	What About the Children?	88
8.	The Aftermath	94
9.	Your New Life	100
	Useful Addresses	110
	Index	111

This book is dedicated to my friend Phyllis Morison, with love and gratitude for our many years of friendship.

INTRODUCTION

This book is specifically designed for people who are contemplating divorce, in the throes of divorce, or in the process of recovering from it. Few people contemplating marriage are either sufficiently cautious, or sufficiently cynical, to read a book about its failure beforehand — although knowing why marriages break down and how such a situation can sometimes be avoided, might very well prove helpful and even preventive.

I should add that you will learn far more from its pages about how to help yourself — and your children if you have them — through the acute emotional upheaval of divorce than you will about the legal aspects of the process. We shall look at why — and how — divorce occurs; how it is sometimes possible to steer a marriage through a difficult course on rough seas, avoiding its being shattered on the rocks of mutual hatred and resentment; and what to do about the situation if the damage proves irreversible.

What I am immediately about to say has been said so many times before that, in repeating it, I may justifiably be accused of using a cliché. But it is a demonstrable fact that life *does* exist on the other side of the Divorce Court, and so too do love and liberty, if you can summon up the courage to pursue them. Becoming divorced can mark the start of a new and happier era in your life which gives you the space and the freedom gradually to rebuild your shattered self-confidence and to form satisfying relationships. And it can provide the peace and freedom from stress that you may well have lacked for years.

On the other hand, divorce itself is very often the most traumatic experience, other than bereavement, that a man or woman can go through. And material deprivation — even severe financial hardship — can prove an added burden. Before dealing with the subject in depth, however, it is worth taking a close look at the institute of marriage and trying to determine its meaning for us in today's society.

For divorce is the unequivocal destruction of a mutually constructed edifice; and before we participate, willingly or unwillingly, in this process, it is sensible to understand a little of how, and why, we built it in the first place. Just as there are many life forms on this planet, so there are many forms of death; and every time a house is pulled down, a battered car transported to the scrap yard, or old furniture piled in a heap to which a match is set — an object, dear to someone at some past time, loses its unique existence. If sadness can be associated with this sort of loss, how very much more tragic is the death of a marriage, a relationship which the partners at least in the first instance intend to be a permanent one. It is only when the edifice of our marriage has crumbled irreparably, and become unfit for human habitation, that we should set about its systematic destruction. And once we have set ourselves such an unpleasant task — or had the job involuntarily foisted upon us — it simply makes sense to approach it with the minimum risk of self-injury and none whatever of self-annihilation.

1.

WHY MARRIAGE?

Why ever marry in the first place? Why do we, in common with people in many other societies, take marriage for granted? The origins of the first formal marriage are lost in the mists of antiquity. It was certainly recognized throughout the ancient world, as we know from extant writings from the pre-Christian era, Egyptian, Roman and Greek to mention only the familiar few. Couples within these civilizations were formally united, at least among the upper echelons of society, and the union solemnized by some kind of a ceremony presided over by a ritual priest figure. The formalizing of marriage, was not confined to mere mortals; the very gods themselves were formally paired in connubial bliss, an occasion which often demanded the blessings of the presiding deity, as well as celebration, feasting, laughter and rejoicing.

Two characteristics feature again and again in marriage ceremonies through the ages. One is the religious aspect, despite the many variants of religious belief nurtured from race to race and from age to age. The second is that, whether regarded as monogamous or polygamous, the marital state has usually been accepted to be lasting. Vows have been sworn before the deity or his earthly representative, and these have generally been held to be binding except under certain circumstances. In fact, Matthew the Evangelist voiced the opinion of many races throughout the ages when he said 'What therefore God has joined together, let no man put asunder' (19, vi). Even the great St Paul, whose contempt for womankind is legendary and who stated 'To be carnally minded, is death' (Romans, 8, vi), advised 'Let Love be, without dissimulation', and conceded that 'It is better to marry than to burn!'

While much could be said on the topic of monogamy versus polygamy, this is not the place to enter into arguments for or against either. For we are engaged here in taking a look at how marriage is regarded in the West, which is strictly a state of monogamy. But it *is* undeniably pertinent to ask the question 'Is man's nature suited to a monogamous lifestyle?' And if, on reverting from the general to the particular, one asks oneself the question 'Am *I* monogamous by inclination?' — and discovers that the answer is 'No, not really!' then it is safer not to contemplate marriage in the first place.

The reason, of course, is that you are very unlikely to find a marital partner who is not only polygamous him- or herself, but is also quite happy to allow you to be. Clearly the honest answer to the question 'Can one man/woman really ever fulfil all the emotional and physical needs of his/her partner, throughout a lifetime of committed relationship?', must at least initially be 'No'. But it is a qualified negative. Many hundreds of thousands of marriages can — and do — succeed throughout a lifetime of total fidelity on behalf of both husband and wife. And if, either through experience or scepticism, you immediately find yourself questioning the quality of lives lived on those terms, it must be admitted that many of the people living them are very happy indeed.

It is true that complete commitment to a marital partner for 'as long as you both shall live' is an immense undertaking demanding more compromises and greater unselfishness than many of us are capable of. Nevertheless, the fact remains, that for most people there is happiness to be found in pursuing the old-fashioned ideal of an exclusive one-to-one relationship. Marriage protects children legally, should the partners later divorce or one partner die intestate. And a certain amount of financial security is afforded to the wife who, despite recent changes in the law, is still usually able to claim maintenance.

From the financial point of view each working partner in a marriage is, at least in theory, offered greater financial security than would be the case if he or she depended on a single income. Pooling resources generally means that mortgages and Hire Purchase arrangements are easier to obtain, a larger number of luxuries can be afforded and, under certain circumstances of employment or self-employment, a better tax deal from the Inland Revenue can be obtained.

Practical advantages are appealing, too. For, despite the phenomenon of role-reversal which is now a common feature of our age, the majority of married people are not obliged at one and the same time to fulfil the domestic duties of house-person and stay-at-home parent *and* those of provider, defender and breadwinner. Life for the single parent who finds him- or herself attempting to fulfil every role, is frequently very hard indeed, and these are problems that are often underestimated both by parents who separate or divorce and by women who elect to have babies and to bring them up without support from the father.

There are, too, the factors of sexual and emotional satisfaction which prompt many of us to marry. It is true that fidelity bars us from the excitement of pursuing and winning a succession of sexual partners. But the other side of the coin from the attractions of multiple choice, is the satisfaction of living with a permanent sexual partner who is — at least when the marriage is a happy one — both attractive to us and capable of sharing sexual experience in a mutually satisfying way. George Bernard Shaw attributed the popularity of marriage to the fact that 'It combines the maximum of temptation with the maximum of opportunity', and there is a lot to be said for being able to rely on a little (or for that matter, a lot of!) sexual dalliance over a rainy weekend.

The emotional benefits mentioned here in association with marriage are obviously just as applicable to people who live together on a permanent basis — even if many men and women who have done just this and have later decided to marry, finally admit that there is 'something special' about the married state and that for some reason they both feel more secure as a result of having entered into it. Just as a marriage certificate is a totally inadequate means of binding people together once they have ceased to love one another, so, too, it cannot be taken as representing the inmost meaning of married life. But in this chapter we are taking a brief look at the conventional married state so that the rest of the book can better deal with its dissolution.

Besides the sexual benefits of being married, there is, too, the simple domestic satisfaction of setting up a home with one's partner, an activity which appeals to some of our most basic instincts. And however frugal or sophisticated such a home built together might be, it is likely ultimately to contain many signs of a happily shared experience; such as children's toys, unsightly wedding presents from dearly loved elderly relatives, and familiar though financially worthless souvenirs of places visited together — unlike the homes of many determinedly single people, which sometimes contain expensive symbols of consciously acquired style and continuing independence. Such abodes often fail to feel welcoming or 'lived in', perhaps because those who live alone and for themselves alone, at times try far too hard to impress.

These then, are a few of the reasons why the majority of us choose both a monogamous way of life and the blessings, if not of the Church, then at least of the State. What are the alternatives?

As pointed out above, the 'marriage of two minds' which binds many people together for a lifetime of commitment, is the emotional equivalent of legalized marriage and within this context may be considered as synonymous with it. This leaves as the true alternatives: living alone and avoiding romantic and sexual relationships of all kinds; living alone, and having a lengthy love relationship with a man or woman which does not culminate in a shared lifestyle but which may well be, at least on the side of one of the participants, monogamous; and living alone and having a series of on-off affairs, one-night stands, or several concomitant casual affairs.

There is also communal living, but this does tend to be outside the experience (and indeed beyond the capability) of most of us. And even within the context of a commune, people tend to pair up and form stable relationships which are just as likely to become permanent, dissolve under stress or become subjected to the pressures of fear, misunderstanding and jealousy, as those formed under more conventional conditions.

What do these alternatives to marriage have to offer those who choose them? Let's start by taking a look at living alone without any kind of emotional involvement. Those who do so from choice either enjoy being self-sufficient in this way, or for some reason within their past experience are so determined never to become involved emotionally with anyone again that their own company is all they really wish for. I have great respect for the person who decides to 'go it alone' although I do think that to do so as a result of bitterness and mistrust of other human beings is very sad — and I am not being the slightest bit patronizing when I say so.

Those who genuinely wish to avoid close human contact are relatively rare; for the sex instinct is so developed in nearly everyone that immense frustration results from its repression and an outlet has to be sought for its relief. Some apparently lonely individuals who are pitied by their acquaintances, and even by members of their family, as being 'unable to form close relationships' are in fact gay (homosexual) and do not choose to make the fact known to those whom they feel would not understand. And while you can feel a great deal of admiration for gay people who *do* 'come out' and live life as they choose, it is not difficult to understand what motivates other gay people to keep quiet about their sexual preferences.

Some 'loners', then, are simply doing exactly what they seem to be doing, which is pursuing the lifestyle they feel best fits them. Many *are* suspected — quite incorrectly — of being gay, while in fact they have an unusually low level of libido (sexual energy) and prefer the peace, quiet and lack of complication of a single lifestyle. Other lone people are patronized and pitied by those who know them, while in fact they are gay and having a whale of a time behind everyone's back! And if they occasionally smile to themselves with the thought 'If only they knew, they would stop trying to pair me off with someone of the opposite sex', you really can't blame them.

One of my patients springs to mind in this context. Gabriel, as I shall call him, was the extremely good-looking managing director of an industrial chemicals plant. He very rarely had anything wrong with his health, but I used to see him from time to time when he required vaccinations before his frequent trips abroad. I had never been asked to visit him at home, so was not aware that he lived alone, although I knew there was no wife of the same name among our patients.

One day he came to see me in quite a state. He asked me if we could chat, and it seemed that his secretary who had been with him for years, had left. The 'temp.', moreover, who had been engaged in his absence while a new permanent secretary was being sought, had developed a heavy crush on him. To make matters worse, he told me, there would be lots of business functions which he would have to attend, and to which he had always taken his previous secretary, a nice, safe, middle-aged lady who was his elder by about fifteen years. Now he would have either to attend functions alone, or go through the motions of inviting a girl out for the purpose — a thought which clearly horrified him.

Doctors must always know when to be outspoken and when to keep quiet, and on this occasion I obeyed my instinct and asked Gabriel whether he was gay. He looked immensely relieved and admitted at once that he was.

> The problem is, doctor, I dare not let anyone know at work, it would be terrible. It's bad enough that my colleagues know I live alone — I mean, I keep having to invent girlfriends and torrid affairs and married mistresses and things. I have a perfectly satisfactory lifestyle, and wouldn't become 'straight' even if that were possible; but it is a terrible nuisance to have to keep pretending.

I reassured him as much as I could and suggested that he continue as before, but give the devoted 'temp.' a bonus and a superb reference and send her back from whence she came. I also put it to him that, as his old secretary had had to leave the company because arthritis was affecting her typing, it might be a good idea to ask her whether she would care to continue to accompany him to important functions. Gabriel thought this was a very good suggestion, especially as she had been with him for so long that he believed she knew, or could guess, about his private life. This gesture would also be a tacit statement of his refusal to pretend any longer, to a greater degree than was absolutely necessary, about girlfriends, his mythical sex life and so on.

The plan certainly worked, and he even managed to get Miss Jenkins, his old secretary, to come in a few days a week in a managerial capacity, leaving nearly all the typing to a proficient office junior. Gabriel continued to take Miss Jenkins to office functions, too; and, to give his colleagues their due, no questions were ever asked nor comments made, at least within his hearing, of the reasons for these changes.

With respect to sad and bitter people who shut themselves off from close association with others, I would venture to advise them to consider giving life another chance. Certainly some experiences of ill-matched relationships are enough to make the idea of another close involvement repugnant. This may have happened to you. But however you feel, don't cut yourself off from people completely; extend a little friendship and see whether it works. When you feel safe — extend a little more. And do mix socially with both your own sex and the opposite one. Neither man nor woman is an island and if you attempt to live like one life can be dreadfully lonely.

A medical colleague of mine had a patient like this; she had been a battered wife and had left her husband three times, only to return home because on each occasion he found out where she was staying and threatened to kill her unless she went back to live with him. Finally (and I must say, thankfully for her), her brute of a husband was jailed for twenty years for robbery with violence and attempting to shoot a police officer. So at last Annette left her old home where such terrible scenes and beatings had occurred and took a job as a live-in cook, a job for which she had been trained.

However, she was adamant that she would never have anything to do with a man again, and shut herself away in her rooms whenever she was not on duty. One morning her employer knocked on her door as she had not prepared breakfast, and opened it to discover her unconscious in bed, having taken a bottle of sleeping tablets, a half bottle of brandy and some aspirin. She survived this tragic attempt to end her own life, and although not many lives as sad as this one have very happy endings — Annette's did. Her employer's wife died while Annette was convalescing and when she returned to her job, a sympathy slowly grew between her and the grieving widower.

After much nervous deliberation she finally plucked up courage and not only divorced her husband but also married Mark. They now have twin boys, and are extremely happy. One significant point, though, is that Annette never attempted suicide all the time she lived with her first violent husband. Life was hell for her, but she was not without human contact even though the contact she experienced was of a highly undesirable kind. It was not until she deliberately cut herself off from human social contact apart from that which her job involved, that her will to survive finally succumbed.

Do many people form close emotional/sexual ties with others and yet never actually have the satisfaction of sharing life fully with them?

A fair number of people live this kind of life, and while it is rarely safe to make sweeping statements, particularly about human relationships, I think I am safe in saying that affinities of this type are rarely satisfactory, nor productive of much happiness. Many single men and women at some point in their lives, have a married lover — and unless the affair is kept successfully casual by both parties (and this is very difficult to achieve), both people suffer and the one usually in the worse position is the unattached person.

This is not to say that it cannot prove equally painful for the married partner, and it is almost always more difficult and worrying for him/her if the unsuspecting husband or wife is to be kept in the dark — which is usually the case. Such affairs are generally temporary, however, as the strain of deceit grows too much and the married person finds the burden of guilt too heavy. The unmarried lover, on the other hand, grows weary and saddened by lonely Christmasses, Bank holidays and weekends, and the knowledge that his or her lover can never spend even the night with them, unless elaborate precautions are taken beforehand.

For these reasons many such relationships come to an end. They can offer excitement, and relief either from the tedium of a lonely existence or the boredom of a less-than-ideal marriage. When the attached person is able to spend reasonable periods of time with his or her mistress or lover, the semblance of a shared domestic life can be reached. But a relationship such as this rarely offers either person sufficient satisfaction for them to wish to pursue it in the long run.

On the other hand, a very few people are content to see their lovers occasionally rather than all the time or even every day. For certain types of temperament a mixture of the single life and the shared is exactly right, and as both participants are happy, such a relationship may well take the place of marriage and last throughout a lifetime.

Rather more frequently, though, there exists a much less than ideal state of affairs in which the married partner is unwilling or unable to 'let go' of the other, while never seriously considering divorcing his or her own spouse. Typically, the unmarried person is by far the more deeply attached of the two, and may well end up spending many years of his or her life in struggling unsuccessfully against a relationship which has become an obsession. All hope of marriage, a shared life and children are lost; and yet the individual clings to the clandestine meetings with the selfish lover as to life itself.

It is very difficult to counsel such people, for they come to ask for advice and yet will not hear a word of criticism against the loved one, nor contemplate for a moment relinquishing him or her. Suzie G. was one such patient, who came to my counselling clinic requesting sleeping pills just before a Bank holiday weekend. I knew she had a history of depression so I asked her why she wanted them and she revealed the real reason — she intended to blot out the interval of time between Friday night and Tuesday morning, by continuous sleep. 'I cannot bear to remain conscious,' she told me in a barely audible voice. 'Frank is taking his wife and the two children abroad for four days and it kills me to know they are all together. I cannot bear to be alive and not have him — *and* know that he is with someone else. Even if he *is* married to her.'

I asked her gently what she considered to be the quality of her daily life when there was no Bank holiday weekend looming; and she burst into tears and said she felt suicidal. She had been faithful to Frank ever since she met him at the age of eighteen; he had been her boss then, and they had fallen in love. Many times he had told her that he would never leave his wife Kitty for her; but he never broke the relationship off completely.

As an emergency measure I got her to agree to spend the Bank holiday with her mother in Portsmouth, and to accept a sicknote, stating that she was unfit to attend work — which she was. She needed a lot of encouragement, but I managed to persuade her to write a note to Frank ending the relationship, and spend an extended period of four weeks on a farm, out in the open and among friends, where she could find plenty of hard physical work to do and have as little time as possible to grieve.

Not all counselling is so well heeded as this was, though she did break down once and 'phone Frank who fortunately was out. In the end, the fresh-air routine worked extremely well as I was certain it would, given the chance. Suzi was thirty at the time of the crisis, and she began to realize that she had given Frank twelve precious years of her life. Barn dances and the Harvest Home featured in Suzi's four week stay, and she was a different person when I saw her a week after her return. 'I've met a super student farmer down in Devon,' she admitted with a shy smile, 'and he [Roger] wants me to go back and work there permanently so that we can be together. His agricultural college is not far away and he works on the farm every weekend as well.' I was delighted for her, and also very pleased that she had ignored three letters from the deserted Frank.

Some people are stuck with this sad substitute for a marriage for a lifetime; but Suzi was one of the lucky (and plucky) ones. She broke with Frank, never to return, and married her student farmer a year later.

Most people in our society, then, seek some sort of a marriage or marriage substitute, and this can even be said of people like Suzi who know that within the confines of their present relationship a real marriage is not possible. Characteristically they make their home as cosy and welcoming as possible — probably wishing to create the illusion of happy married life whenever their lover *is* free to spend some time with them. Men and women who opt for a lifetime of shortlived affairs, however, are often afraid of permanent commitment and all that marriage implies, and prefer a series of brief (even staccato) relationships which will not result in any lasting emotional bonding.

Most people have some type of premarital sex and a number of casual affairs, but this is not the same thing at all as the studied avoidance of close relationships and the indulgence in one-night stands strictly as a means of proving sexual prowess and obtaining sexual relief. A fair number of men — and women — who suffer from depression and/or request counselling or psychotherapy, are those very people who have lived the most enviable and exciting lives earlier on — as far as the rest of the world is concerned, anyway.

Peter R. was one such patient. Aged thirty-nine and starting to look a little prematurely middle-aged, he came to me for depression and sleeplessness which surprised me as he was a well-known name locally — and always seemed to be living the 'high life', wining and dining the prettiest girls, jetting to romantic places and generally being referred to as the most eligible bachelor around.

'It's not really much fun,' he admitted, wearily. 'I'm nearly forty, all my friends are married and have kids — something I'd like — and I am still tearing all over the place at an incredible speed. I must have slept with fifty girls and older women, at least. And I don't think I've ever felt a thing for one of them.'

I recommended psychotherapy on a twice weekly basis for Peter, as he was getting fairly seriously depressed and starting to drink. My husband, who is a hypnotherapist and counsellor, saw him — and he came to report to me once a month during surgery hours. Fortunately he did not need antidepressant drugs and six months of hypnoanalysis and therapy helped Peter a good deal. I must stress that we have failures as well as successes among those we counsel and advise; but, as it happens, Peter responded very well, and ended by marrying a very ordinary, very dear girl twelve years his junior whom he had known all her life.

Marriage — or some form of an equally binding relationship — seems to attract most people finally, even though many of us have to work our way through varying phases of sexual relationship and life experiences before we reach the stage at which we are ready for final and binding commitment.

To err is, unfortunately for us, only too human; and with the best intentions in the world, mistakes are made. Marriages are entered into that prove to be a hell of confusion and mutual misery rather than the heaven of happiness and contentment we hope for. And we have to end them.

No marriage, in my opinion, is worth preserving for the sake of what relatives, friends and neighbours might say; for financial reasons alone; or even for the sake of children, provided they can be made happy and secure with one or other parent. We must now look at how the eternal bonds of the marriage contract can either be coaxed asunder — or, if no alternative exists — how they can be prised apart to release the captives held in bondage between them, waiting to escape into the freedom of their separate ways.

2.

WHY DIVORCE?

Current statistics show that one marriage in every three in Britain ends in the Divorce Court. Many reasons are put forward to account for this high rate, including teenage marriages, unemployment and redundancy, the influence of the media, and the easy availability of divorces. There certainly are many contributory factors, but I think that the last mentioned needs to be qualified.

On the surface, the fact that divorce from one's marital partner is relatively easy to achieve, obviously augments the total annual divorce figure; but it does not *cause* the actual divorces to take place. The divorce itself is the legal termination of a contract between two people to live together as man and wife. What needs to be considered is the reason why so many marriages break down in the first place. There could be an element of truth in the claim that people try less hard to preserve their marriages since easy divorce is always available. But one wonders how many marriages were just as unhappy as many are today, in the days when divorce was practically unheard of.

Let's look at the various aspects of life today that *are* blamed, with a certain amount of justification, for contributing to the high divorce rate, and see whether they have a common factor.

Teenage Marriages
It is now possible to marry at the age of sixteen with the consent of a parent or guardian, and at eighteen without anyone's consent. To do so is not necessarily to court disaster, for it is perfectly possible to meet and match up with a partner in your teens with whom you wish to stay for the rest of your life. It is prejudiced to say, for example, that *because* John is seventeen and Ann is sixteen, their marrying in the very near future is bound to be a mistake and to end in divorce. But the sad fact remains — as any concerned parent is bound to point out — that few girls and boys in their mid- to late teens *are* mature enough to decide whom they are going to marry.

It is certain that youngsters of that age fall very heavily in love. Films and television, comics and magazines, books, advertising techniques and most entertainment aimed at the teenage market encourage their readers or target audience to match and mate at the earliest opportunity — and suggest subtly the superiority of the pair over the single individual. Teenagers accept this idea easily enough, for the importance of belonging to a group — and by that token, avoiding the inherent oddness of the lone individual — is a dominant factor in children's social structure.

It is a short step from serious dating on a regular basis to planning to marry. For the teenage boy, this seems the ideal way of securing his girl from the clutches of rival males, and of establishing his adulthood with the status of husband and protector, and probably of father as well. For the girl in her mid-to late teens, for whom there may be no hope of further education and very little of employment, marriage and starting a family offer the opportunity of a familiar role, and the hope, at least in the future, of financial security.

This is only looking at the practical side of the issue. There is, of course, the overriding feeling of being deeply in love and of wanting to 'secure' that feeling by marriage in the face of an uncertain future. The teenage years are very much a time for sorting out, rejecting and establishing ideas; this in part accounts for rebelliousness at school and at home, and disagreements with authority figures generally. If you add together the various aspects of the argument in favour of teenage marriage, from the participants' point of view, it is not difficult to see why so many teenage marriages take place.

With respect to poor employment prospects and the threat of future redundancy, these factors do not exert a deterrent influence on the majority of teenagers wishing to get married. There is always the prospect of the dole, with which they may very likely already be acquainted, the possibility of a council flat either straightaway or in the not too distant future, and often the chance to stay at a low rent with either parents or parents-in-law in the meantime.

Problems start when the glamour of the wedding, often achieved in the face of considerable opposition, starts to wear off. With one, or perhaps both, of the married couple out of work and dependent on social security, the high cost of food and rent, petrol, bus fares, clothes and entertainment strike home forcefully. The reality of life in cramped accommodation with no money to spare contrasts dismally with life at home where more than likely washing and ironing, clean bed linen, food, drink and pocket money were provided by one or other parent. And rows frequently start when each person in the new marriage starts to feel trapped — and to blame his or her partner for their own dissatisfaction.

Sadly, the arrival of the first baby under these conditions is far more likely to make matters worse than to bring the young parents closer together. Initially things may improve, especially when delighted grandparents bring gifts and admiration and vie with one another to baby-sit. But as soon as the novelty wears off and the burden of disturbed nights, dirty nappies and frequent feeds is added to the already unsatisfactory domestic picture it is a short step to serious quarrelling, separation and ultimately divorce.

Although as a doctor it is very easy to see all the arguments in favour of the contraceptive Pill and its easy availability, for sex education in schools, and for a healthier, less inhibited attitude to sex generally, one must not forget the other side of the picture. For when our society and the amenities it has to offer, encourage the formation of early sexual relationships, it is only to be expected that teenagers will tend to want to marry and start families before they are emotionally mature enough to make such a choice.

However, while there is doubtless much truth in the old saying: 'Marry in haste and repent at leisure', there are many other reasons for marriages breaking down. The same chain of events as those typically affecting teenage marriages, can affect marriages between older people, too. For cramped living conditions, a shortage of money, several young children making their demands and the constant fear of redundancy pose stresses that prove too much for many partnerships to withstand.

Redundancy and Unemployment
Great pressure is exerted upon a marital relationship when one or other partner is unemployed or made redundant. If this affects a wife, whose salary normally plays an important role in the home economy, then the domestic budget is stretched to the limit. If this is managed successfully, then life is hard enough with no extra cash available for luxuries, treats or 'extras'. If the situation is managed unsuccessfully, then to the already strained financial situation and the deprivations which that imposes, are added the constant worry of bills which cannot be paid, unpleasant letters threatening court action, and maybe even visits from the bailiff.

The same situation affects the family, of course, if the husband's job is the one to be lost or to fail to materialize; but in this instance there are often attendant psychological problems with which to contend. The husband is even more likely than his wife to feel resentful at being unemployed, both because this is in itself demoralizing, and because he is unlikely to enjoy staying at home 'minding the baby' while his wife plays the part of breadwinner.

Anger and self-blame remain the average man's most probable response to 'being kept' by his wife, despite the frequency with which role reversal in a marriage is actually chosen nowadays as a way of life. And, paradoxically, the husband's self-directed anger often finds an outlet in direction, instead, towards his wife and family. This is one of the reasons why some men who are 'on the dole' and already short of money, spend what little they have on drink, betting and gambling. Rows very naturally arise at home when the working wife finds herself supplying pocket money intended for the pub, a game of cards or the racecourse — and such quarrels frequently become violent. It is not difficult to see how this situation leads to mutual dislike.

A thirty-year-old patient of mine, called Carol, came for marital counselling for this very reason. She worked as an accounts clerk, and her job was the only current source of family finance since her husband had been made redundant. She asked for advice, for what had once been a happy marriage was rapidly disintegrating into a hell of violence and bitter words. Len, her husband, accused her of 'snootiness' and even infidelity because she refused to give up her job and join the dole queue — to make him feel better about being out of work!

He had already hit her twice and although he had not physically harmed her she was not prepared to stay with him if he repeated the action. Unfortunately, before we were able to sort out some kind of a solution to the problem (which would have involved Len coming to see us for counselling), Carol learned from an acquaintance at work that her husband was spending the few pounds he had each week on buying her best friend drinks and taking her to the cinema.

Carol packed her bags that very evening and started divorce proceedings the following day.

Illness — Physical and Mental
I include illness among my major causes of divorce with a certain amount of trepidation, since so many hundreds of marriages remain happy and stable in the face of severe illness of one or other partner, or of one of the children. But chronic ill-health poses a severe strain upon the family unit regardless of which family member is afflicted — and marriages that remain happy despite the fact must certainly be blessed by extra strength.

When sickness affects the wife and mother, the husband has the problem of running the home and looking after the children, either alone or with external help if she has to go to hospital, or under her direction if she is confined to bed at home. If the latter is the case, some of the puzzles of managing domestic affairs may be solved for him, but he may also have to care for his sick wife into the bargain. The man as a husband may be loving and devoted, and genuinely wish to care for his afflicted wife; but this may necessitate giving up his job in order to do so, or working overtime on a regular basis in order to pay for assistance.

Whichever is the case, the strain can become intolerable. The same applies to the wife caring for a sick husband, and trying to cope with one or several young children and perhaps a job as well, and the psychological strain on the sick person must not be underestimated. Chronic illness often brings the added burden of depression and hopelessness — and while the reasons why these arise are easy to understand, they do nothing to lighten the load of either the patient or his or her partner.

The presence of mental illness in a partner can, in fact, be a lot harder to come to terms with than physical illness. With the numbers of psychiatric patients today far exceeding the country's resources for caring for them, as many mentally sick people as possible are looked after at home. This has several advantages for the patient, since hospitalization can have a detrimental effect upon mentally sick people and retard rather than hasten their recovery. But a severely depressed or phobic husband or wife is by no means easy to look after; and if the illness is even more complex the task can make life almost impossibly hard.

Theresa was forty-two when she joined my general practice panel, and all we knew about her husband at first was that he was a chronic invalid, as his notes were late in reaching us and Theresa was reluctant to talk about him. Then one night, just before the Relief Service was due to take over, we had a call to the Fosters' house, to see Fred Foster 'as an emergency'.

Theresa met us at the door and told us that Fred had been 'taken funny' again. He had, in fact, hit the kids, threatened his wife with a chopper, and then locked himself in their bedroom threatening to hang himself from one of the ceiling beams. The police had to be called, and Fred extricated and sent to a mental hospital 'under a section' — which means that we utilized section twenty-nine of the Mental Health Act. This enables a minimum of two doctors to send a patient to a psychiatric hospital against his or her will — where the patient will be retained for varying periods of time according to the response to treatment. For the truth of the matter was that Fred Foster was a paranoid schizophrenic, known to be dangerous at times, and that throughout twenty-two years of marriage

Theresa had cared for him, moving house several times during that period when Fred's outbursts became known and talked about locally.

He had been in and out of hospital many times in the course of his illness and, unfortunately, was not very responsive to treatment. Theresa worked and was able to pay for her two children to go to a boarding school; but the worry of what Fred might do to them during the school holidays made her life a misery. She had no intention of ever leaving her husband who was, she told me, the sweetest, gentlest person imaginable 'between bouts'. The main problem was that the start of bouts was unpredictable and this in itself was a further source of mental strain for her.

Illness in a child is a source of worry and stress to both father and mother. All children get sick, but when the illness is serious and prolonged or even fatal, the mental strain and emotional suffering involved can be tremendous. Extra nursing care, special dietary requirements and sometimes private treatment, all pose an extra strain upon the family finance, and sometimes necessitate the mother of a young family going out to work to provide extra cash, and possibly the father seeking extra work or overtime as well. When even these strenuous efforts fail to achieve the desired result, the resultant frustration and guilt can be overwhelming.

Lastly, caring for an elderly relative can sadly contribute to marital breakdown. This is not difficult to understand, when you consider that the stress of caring for a senile or incontinent old person can change a normally stable and loving man or woman into a violent, abusive neurotic requiring mental care him- or herself.

This is how the syndrome of 'granny battering' comes about, and the destructiveness of the situation extends to the marriage of those in a caring capacity, the hapless elderly person involved, and often to the children of the marriage who witness abusive treatment and intense domestic misery at an impressionable age. With the present acute shortage of geriatric hospital beds and home nursing facilities, this is a situation which at present seems to have no solution. One can only say that it is *sometimes* in the best interest for everyone concerned for the elderly person to be placed in as pleasant an Old People's

Home as can be found or afforded. However reluctant caring sons and daughters may be to see Mum or Dad in such a place, it is unlikely that the family home would prove a happier place for the old person to end his or her days, if the domestic pressures resulting from such an arrangement were sufficient to threaten the marriage itself.

Infidelity
This remains a frequent cause of marital breakdown and until the law was changed it was one of the few grounds upon which divorce would almost invariably be granted. The reasons why married people are unfaithful to one another are legion, and range from the once-in-a-lifetime mistake to deliberate, open promiscuity.

The former may happen to almost anyone, and result from a drink too many with a business colleague or from an attempt to punish one's partner for some hurtful action. The wife or husband who does have sex with someone else other than their married partner for the first time, generally experiences considerable guilt afterwards and may feel acutely unhappy unless able to 'confess'.

Whatever the pleas put forward by someone in this sort of distress, I invariably counsel them *not* to confess their infidelity to their mate. Of course one of the ideals in married life is complete honesty and freedom of expression, but in practice few marriages *are* ideal and few can withstand the blow that such a confession can deal. This is not to say that there would necessarily be an imminent threat of divorce. But the only good that such an admission can achieve is the release of pent-up guilt on behalf of the unfaithful partner. The harm it can cause can be indiscernible at first, and the matter appear to be forgiven and forgotten. But it is unwise to sow the seeds of doubt and disillusion in the mind of one's husband or wife. Better to ride out the period of guilt, the discomfort of which *does* diminish with time, than to risk the destruction of faith and mutual trust.

This is what Shakespeare's Othello says when the satanic Iago has persuaded him that Desdemona's virtue is in doubt:

> O! now for ever
> Farewell the tranquil mind; farewell content!
> Farewell the plumed troop and the big wars
> That make ambition virtue! O farewell! . . .

Othello was never to know another moment of mental peace, and his mental turmoil resulted from suspicion alone which was completely without foundation. A mighty military leader, he bade farewell to all other aspects of life which had held meaning for him, once he believed that he had reason to mistrust his blameless wife. And the tragedy ends by his murdering her.

Histrionic and vastly overdramatized by today's standards, you might say. But violent deeds do stem from jealousy and mistrust, even in the mildest of people, and it is foolish to risk the foundations of your marriage being shattered because of the urge to release pent-up feeling. If you find yourself in this position, go and talk with a marriage guidance counsellor, a minister, your parents or a trustworthy best friend. And comfort yourself with the thought that you are causing no-one any unnecessary pain.

At the other end of the spectrum, there is the happy-go-lucky arrangement in which both partners agree to go their separate ways and take lovers as and when they choose. I am not denying the possibility of this working well for a small minority of people; but I am always most suspicious when one or other partner of such an arrangement claims that they are wonderfully happy. However easily some married people can countenance their own sexual adventures, it is a fact of human nature that the same taste for adventuring is far less palatable in one's husband or wife.

Women no longer have to accept — as they did before the advent of the sexual revolution — that two standards of sexual permissiveness exist, a liberal one for their menfolk and a morally strict one for themselves. This is one of the benefits of the new, liberal attitude to sexuality which began to develop in the early 1960s.

Between these two extremes — the guilt-ridden, once only person and the overtly promiscuous one — comes the run-of-the-mill man or woman involved in a moderately happy marriage, who may have an affair or two during his or her lifetime. This, even if discovered, is unlikely to cause an unbreachable rift between husband and wife; but if for some other reason, the marriage does come to an untimely end, infidelity is usually brought up by the party suing for divorce.

The point worth noting here is that even the stability of a mediocre marriage between two people who do not appear to care very deeply for one another, can be lastingly affected by infidelities which do not seem to make their mark at the time that they occur.

Divergent Interests
Most reasonably mature people realize that considerable effort is required for two people to live together harmoniously; so the majority of newly married people succeed in adapting to one another's different lifestyles, even though the existence of such differences may present quite a shock when first recognized.

This is because part of being in love is the feeling of total union with one's mate, so much so that the ideal of 'one in flesh, and one in spirit' becomes a reality. Personal habits may differ considerably though, and pass unnoticed, especially when the couple live separately before they marry — and readjustments have to be made to encompass, say, the wife's extreme tidiness in contrast to her husband's unbelievable untidiness.

More serious than minor differences in domestic habits, is a pronounced divergence of interests. It sometimes happens that a seriously courting or engaged couple will be so anxious to please one another with respect to dates, outings, choice of entertainment, even views on life, religious beliefs and the important question of having a family, that each forms a totally false impression of the other's tastes.

Bernard and Molly are two newly-weds who come immediately to mind in this context. They came for counselling because they felt they were drifting apart. During their eleven months of engagement, they had been to the opera a total of eleven times! Molly was insane about grand opera — and was quite justified in supposing that Bernard was, too, for he had willingly bought tickets for every performance she had voiced an interest in, and had even arranged a box at the first night performance of a new production of *Tosca*, in celebration of their engagement.

Now, married for eighteen months and with their first baby on the way, it seemed that Bernard very much preferred sport to operatic performances and had steadily declined to go to a single performance ever since the wedding. 'Quite honestly, doctor,' he volunteered, 'I cannot bear serious singing — at the most I can endure a Gilbert and Sullivan performance once a year at Christmas. I don't understand German or French or Italian — so what is the point? In any case I am tone deaf!'

I had to suppress a smile — because I was in exactly the same situation as a medical student when I fancied the Best Voice in College and went to all manner of vocal performances I wouldn't normally have dreamed of attending. However, I had been lucky and had ended up, if not engaged to the Finest Tenor To Qualify In Medicine, at least with an established appreciation of choral music and both light and grand operatic works. Bernard, it seemed, had been playing the same game!

The best advice I could give, was the cultivation of an open mind towards activities one had always thought one loathed, and the practice of forebearance for the sake of love! In this case it worked, for Molly and Bernard had come early enough in the course of their differences for compromises to be made with humour and without resentment.

Counselling did not work so well for another couple, Ray and Judith, who had been married for six years. They had allowed great resentment and even rooted dislike of one another to develop, after discovering shortly after their marriage that their interests were highly divergent — in many respects. Judith liked picnics, Ray enjoyed expense account eating. Judith longed for a family; Ray thoroughly disliked children, to whom he invariably referred as 'brats', and wouldn't consider having a family at any price. Moreover, Judith was an agnostic while Ray was Scottish Presbyterian; Judith was a born optimist while her husband was a doleful, complaining pessimist; and, worst of all, so far as they were concerned (with the exception of the question of children), Judith was exquisitely tidy, whereas Ray was almost slum-like in the way he left the bathroom, sink and bedroom, and complained continually about what he called Judith's 'cleaning fetish'.

I was trying to decide where to begin with the complex problem of counselling the two of them, when Judith ran off with an old boyfriend from college with whom, it seemed, she had a great deal in common. This was a sad end to a marriage, but possibly best under the circumstances of such entirely divergent interests.

Sexual Problems

The majority of couples marrying during the past ten years, will probably find sexual differences less of a problem than couples who have been married for longer. With today's customary sexual freedom, most people getting engaged and married nowadays at least know that they have sexual tastes in common.

This was not always the case. When it was the exception rather than the rule to make love fully before marriage, some unpleasant surprises ensued when newly married couples discovered one another's sexual proclivities. This difference in sexual preference could lie anywhere between the extremes of a simple difference in libido levels on the one hand, and the challenge of heterosexuality versus homosexuality on the other.

Sexual differences continue to pose problems, however. Typical situations in which it can be expected to arise, are the planned marriages of the Indian caste system, and marriages of fifteen or twenty years standing, in which the middle-aged couples have developed very different attitudes to sexual experience.

Two case histories are the best way of illustrating these points. Nilu and Rashmi Patel came for counselling. He was a wealthy, rotund Indian of forty, married for four months to a tiny, fragile and sexually ignorant seventeen-year-old Indian beauty — by a marriage contract that had been arranged between Rashmi and Nilu's parents some ten years previously. He had had, by his own admission, considerable experience of both Indian and white women, while poor little Nilu was still at school when the marriage took place, at which time she was still completely ignorant of the facts of life.

Rashmi consulted me as he wished to have his wife's frigidity cured. It took a year of intensive psychotherapy to bring Nilu to the point at which her courage permitted her to speak her own mind. She loathed Rashmi and the whole concept of 'arranged marriage'; and wished to go to college, take her 'A' levels and become a dentist! We gave her all the encouragement she needed — and in the end, Rashmi was persuaded to agree to release her by divorce.

Finding her own feet at university, Nilu soon developed enough self-confidence to develop relationships suitable to her personality, which was at the same time both curious and timid. After graduating with honours in dental surgery, Nilu married an Australian veterinary surgeon renowned for his sexual prowess and love of liberated ladies!

Daisy and Ronald are the other couple I want to refer to, to illustrate sexual incompatibility. Daisy came to the surgery complaining of 'soreness down there', while Ronald sought our advice for marital problems unbeknown to Daisy! Ronald, who had worked in the City all his life and been very much in contact with the ways of the world, was as keen on love-making at the age of fifty as he had been at the age of twenty — the age at which he and Daisy had married. Daisy, on the other hand, had never been too keen on 'it', and really felt exempt from that particular duty by the time *she* reached the age of fifty.

Consequently, Ronald was suffering from resentment and frustration, while his wife complained of a persecution complex, depression, sleeplessness and vaginal soreness. I felt the best thing to do was to ask them whether they would be prepared to visit a sex counsellor together. To my surprise Daisy agreed, and I am certain that this was due to her great love for her husband. Contrary to the results sometimes obtained from sex counselling, Daisy and Ron did very well. They attended for a total of eight sessions, and Ron learned to be far more patient and solicitous of Daisy's feelings, while Daisy gradually began to get rid of her dislike and fear of the sex act.

They were ultimately successful in what they set out to do, which was to improve their sexual relations and rid their marriage of the only obstacle ever seriously to have threatened it.

The other side of the coin from the case history of Daisy and Ronald, is that of impotence — and in practice this can pose a greater problem to a relationship than female frigidity. The reason for this is that very many women are prepared to pretend that they enjoy lovemaking, and to fake orgasms — perhaps for the duration of their married lives — and less than astute husbands are none the wiser.

A man who cannot obtain, or who cannot sustain, an

erection, is in a considerably less enviable situation, whatever feminist thinking on the subject states. He does not have the choice of pretending that all is well, and this means that both he and his wife are affected by what is still widely regarded as his 'failure'. Some couples are wise and loving enough to overcome this difficulty together — and in such cases, the problem is usually soon overcome. But when the husband's feelings of frustration and humiliation are augmented by his wife's distress and anxiety, the problem is inevitably compounded.

I should like to stress that I am not necessarily supporting the idea of a wife faking orgasms. Objections to this practice are, first, that it is more likely to lead to resentment, tension and guilt at 'living a lie', than to satisfaction and peace of mind; and second, no sexual problem is likely to right itself unless discussed, shared and approached by both partners. One cannot deny, though, that many frail male egos have been protected from supposed criticism, by loving wives and mistresses utilizing their acting ability in bed — or that this same ploy saves an equal number of vulnerable female egos from the masculine criticism of 'frigidity'. It is a shame ever to have to deceive one's lover in bed; but there are occasions when to admit to lack of satisfaction can be even more harmful.

Sexual problems sufficiently serious to cause real worry and distress should be taken (by both partners) to a sympathetic GP, a marriage guidance counsellor or a Sexual Dysfunction Clinic, which I shall discuss in detail in the next chapter. Ignoring them is likely to be highly injurious, causing unhappiness, anger and frustration.

Sexual problems constitute too big a topic for detailed discussion in this book. But alongside the common ones of female frigidity and male impotence should be mentioned: premature ejaculation; fears associated with masturbation and sexual fantasy; bisexuality, homosexuality and transvestism; and sexual perversion. All of these are capable of posing a threat, grave or trivial depending on the severity, to marital sex; and recognition of their existence, combined with willingness to ask for help, is the *only* way of avoiding permanent damage to a relationship.

Mental and Physical Cruelty

There are as many different varieties of cruelty as there are people capable of its infliction. Its nature and ability to cause damage, is properly recognizable by the couple concerned only, for they alone are aware of the full range of one another's innate susceptibilities. Apart from instances of gross physical abuse, cruelty is also very difficult for an outsider, be he or she the couple's closest friend, to assess, for unerring knowledge of how best to wound, or how paradoxically to please, belongs to the husband and wife and no other.

My meaning is illustrated perfectly by the case of Bertie and Paula. Bertie and Paula were not the type of people to come to a counselling clinic; they were both alcoholics and well known to both the staff in the local Casualty department *and* in the local Police Station. Bertie was always getting blind drunk and bashing Paula who in turn, and equally drunk, would clobber Bertie with the nearest heavy object she could lay her hands on. If either happened to attend surgery alone, to have stitches removed or a tetanus jab, not a word of complaint could ever be extracted against the absent partner and it was obvious that despite the frequent infliction upon one another of grievous bodily harm, they doted upon one another.

I have only on one occasion ever seen either Bertie or Paula in tears, which came as a shock, so inured did they both seem to suffering as the term is generally understood. Bertie came into the surgery one day, and burst into tears. He had no apparent wounds, apart from his usual motley collection of scratches and bruises and only one black eye. 'Do you know what that cow has done?' he bellowed at me, rushing into my consulting room and thumping the desk while I was taking the blood pressure of a timid little man who shrank visibly from such violent language and behaviour. Without pausing for an answer, he yelled for everyone within miles to hear, 'She told me last night, that the first year we was married, she got taken in the family way, and it died before it was born and she's never told me about it, not in thirty years.'

This action of Paula's came about when she started to imagine Bertie fancied one of the nurses in Casualty. She clearly knew his most vulnerable point, and the weapon she should choose in order to inflict most pain. Physical blows amounted to a daily lifestyle with the two of them. But this admission on the part of Paula amounted to serious mental cruelty to Bertie's mind, for it represented disloyalty and secrecy in the one human being of whom he had always felt certain.

The attitude of these two people to physical violence, though, was highly unusual, for the majority of battered wives (and husbands) soon detest their heavy-fisted partner and opt for separation and divorce shortly after the pattern of abuse becomes established. A number of such couples stay together. But this is generally for a reason connected with supporting the children, hoping that the violent behaviour will disappear (which rarely happens), or fear of a worse fate should the victim's whereabouts be discovered.

It is not always possible to conclude that a wife (or husband) is the victim of physical cruelty, however, simply because unmistakable signs of physical violence are apparent. I remember being extremely puzzled once on examining a young, newly married patient named Marian, who appeared to be normally happy and yet whose chest, back, thighs and buttocks were wealed, bruised, grazed and even blistered in three places from cigarette stubs (usually recognizable from the size and shape of the burns).

I was giving her a pre-Pill check, and immediately asked her how she had come by her wounds, all of which looked recently inflicted. She looked at me with a remarkable absence of embarrassment: 'The fact is, Doctor, that Dennis, my husband, gets an incredible kick out of beating and hurting me; and it's lucky he found me, because he would scare the living daylights out of most women. You see, I get an equal thrill out of being hurt, and really we are perfectly happy the way we are, strange as it may seem.'

Happy they may well have been, but I warned Marian severely about the dangers of such 'games' getting out of hand and advised her to draw the line at being burned. She thought about it and agreed, but I suspect that the savage attacks continued because a year later she lost a three month pregnancy 'through tripping and falling downstairs', and left Dennis for another man as soon as she had recovered from the miscarriage.

Child abuse is another type of cruelty capable of destroying a marriage. Usually only one parent is guilty of battering his or her baby or child, and this is often associated with mental sickness or great emotional stress, a marital situation already showing symptoms of collapse, or intolerable domestic circumstances. Great financial strain, cramped and unsuitable living conditions, severe postnatal depression, and the burden of life on the dole, are all factors likely to push a susceptible person in the horrifying direction of physical violence to his or her son or daughter.

It is very difficult indeed for the individual's wife or husband to forgive such an action and, if they are unable to put a stop to their partner's abuse, they have the immediate moral obligation to take steps against it. This obligation at the very least, involves the removal of the child to live temporarily with relatives or friends, and might even result in it being taken into care.

So it is small wonder that child battering is a major factor in marital breakdown, particularly when you consider that both parents are likely to be subject to the same domestic and emotional stresses.

Reluctant Parenthood

Under this heading we must consider both the literally reluctant parents, usually those who are against abortion and opt for marriage in preference to single parenthood and the married couples who *appear* highly reluctant to fulfil a parental role, so inept are they at caring for their offspring.

Marriages contracted purely from a sense of duty to an unborn child are unlikely to succeed. A sense of 'doing the right thing' in the religious or conventional sense may well carry ill-matched partners through the first year of marriage, especially when there is the focal point of the baby's birth. But babies can be disruptive of the closest partnerships, as we saw in the section on Teenage Marriages, and when domestic comfort is destroyed by the demands of a baby both parents may secretly resent, bitter words are often hurled and the blame attached uselessly by each to the other parent.

My advice to people faced with a positive pregnancy test and a feeling of obligation rather than one of love, is to avoid marriage at all costs, for differences and points of incompatibility will become more rather than less apparent as time passes, and need all the affection in the world to overcome. Opt for an abortion if you agree morally with this choice. If not, go ahead with the pregnancy and either determine to keep the child and rear it as a single-parent family with the father having access if mutually agreeable, or put it up for adoption.

This may sound hardhearted; but there is no point in pursuing marriage from a sense of obligation, for all three of you — mother, father and child — are bound to suffer to a certain extent if separation and divorce occur at a later date.

With regard to inefficient parents, most if not all parents are inefficient in a number of ways and there is nothing to worry about in the fact, generally speaking. It is only when the couple are unusually bad at coping with an ordinary and uncomplicated daily existence, that the addition of a baby, or babies, to the domestic stronghold is likely *per se* to have a deleterious effect.

Sandy and Tim are a case in point. Far from being either dull or uneducated, Sandy, aged twenty-two, had graduated from Cambridge a year before the couple became our patients and was the junior partner in a prestigious firm of solicitors. Her husband, Tim, had been to Oxford, and was a qualified marine biologist, but was teaching for the time being since his type of work was somewhat difficult to find in the heart of the metropolis! (Typically, this had never occurred to him when he chose his degree course!)

The couple were not short of money, and as both worked full time they engaged a daily help/nanny to look after their home and one-year-old son while they were out. Sally was a capable 'find' and they grew so dependent upon her management of their homelife that they were utterly bereft when she left to start her own family.

I was called to see Algernon, their little boy, whom they thought to be very ill, and who was in fact cutting a front tooth. Their home, once a delightful oasis of charm and taste in an equally delightful residential area, was an almost incredible sight. Both parents looked utterly distraught, the child was dirty and crying, the house clearly had not been cleaned for weeks — and every single cooking vessel, plate, cup, saucer, glass and item of cutlery they possessed was used, unwashed, and occupying the available space in the kitchen and lounge. Beds were unmade, windows were filthy, at least a month's supply of daily papers and magazines lay on floors and furniture, and the place resembled a gypsies' encampment far more closely than the Bennetts' usually pristine home.

Sandy burst into tears and when I had ascertained what ailed the small patient asked his two parents what had gone wrong. Frankly, neither of them had the slightest idea of how to cope with a child and a home. Running the home unaided would have been more than Sandy was capable of — as she freely admitted; but the presence of a teething baby drove her into paroxysms of panic. Even the amiable marine biologist had seen red! Equally inept, he could not tolerate Sandy's inefficiency and had slapped her face over the breakfast table when she accused him of 'losing' some papers pertaining to one of her clients.

It took a great deal of effort to persuade the pair of them to let Algernon reside for a week with his grandparents; to don jeans and tee-shirts and restore their home to its normal condition; to do an evening course in baby care and household management — *together*; and to attend for counselling.

Alcohol and Drug Dependence

Excessive intake of alcohol by either husband or wife can seriously threaten the stability of a marriage. The extent to which it actually does so depends very much upon the compatibility of the couple's drinking habits, and, where these are vastly different, upon the tolerance and understanding of the partner who drinks the lesser quantity.

If both partners are regular drinkers the chances are reasonably good that the occasional binge on behalf of one of them will be well tolerated by the other. A severe hangover, a vomiting attack — even absence from work and a fine for drunken driving — are more likely to be accepted with sympathy by a husband or wife who also enjoys tippling, than by one who does not. But when one partner enjoys evenings at the pub and boozy parties, while the other is strictly teetotal, even a moderate intake — followed by slight indisposition — can fan the fires of righteous indignation to furnace heat.

More serious, and more likely to bring about a divorce suit, is the case of the habitual drinker married to someone who finds the habit distressing to live with. The man or woman who persists in drinking a considerable amount of alcohol, say a bottle of wine, half a bottle of whisky and five or six pints of beer daily, may well show early signs of deteriorating mentally and physically before the eyes of his or her partner. In addition to this distressing spectacle which the 'dry' spouse has to witness, there is the constant worry of motoring offences, fines and accidents; the possibility of violent behaviour at home or elsewhere; and the unpleasant side-effects that occur to the victim when he or she exceeds the quantity of alcohol to which they have become accustomed.

The dipsomaniac, on the other hand, in contrast to the chronic alcoholic, has drinking bouts during which large volumes of alcohol are imbibed, interspersed with periods either of total abstinence or of very moderate intake. Dipsomaniacs sometimes prove even more distressing to a married partner than chronic drinkers, for at least the habits of the latter are more or less predictable, while the former may appear to respond brilliantly to a 'cure' or drying-out session, then relapse without any warning into their old habits.

Drug addiction is too vast a subject to cover here; suffice it to say that living with a husband or wife who is addicted to a 'hard' and deeply injurious drug places an almost impossible strain on normal marital relations. Physical and mental deterioration may afflict the victim a great deal more swiftly than is the case with the alcohol-dependent person. And added to the appalling knowledge that one's husband or wife is literally killing him- or herself by injecting or swallowing lethal quantities of a dangerous chemical, is the acute and paradoxical anxiety of the substance being unobtainable.

As deadly as alcohol can be, there is at least no criminal offence involved in procuring it. The spouse of the heroin or 'speed' addict lives in fear of a visit from the police, in fear of the addict's withdrawal symptoms should the supply be cut off, and in deadly fear of what the compounds are doing to the life and well-being of the victim. It is not a bit surprising that marriages crumble under the financial and emotional strain of the situation.

A Morbid Adherence to the Past

You will not find this section mentioned in other discussions of factors contributing to divorce, but I have chosen to include it for its particular reference to second marriages.

Not long ago, I was looking through the pages of a women's monthly magazine when I came across an article entitled 'Can Second Marriages Succeed?' I must be honest, and admit that the title gave me a shock. I myself am married for the second time, but one doesn't always draw a parallel between a personal situation and national statistics — and, quite frankly, it had never occurred to me that second marriages ever *did* fail, except of course in the rarest circumstances. And here was an article questioning whether they *ever* work!

Pondering the question I went through our marriage counselling files — and within a half-hour search, extracted four case histories of second marriages which had begun to show signs of floundering. We try to record actual conversations whenever they are particularly relevant to the problem under discussion, and in three of the case histories there was evidence of a common factor.

This factor was a decided dissatisfaction with the present marriage/marital partner, in relation either to what was expected of these two factors or *in relation to the past marriage/marital partner*. And, considering that all parties concerned had been only too glad when their Decrees were made Absolute, it seemed well worth looking into why the present situation had really come about.

Summarizing my findings — and managing to talk to two other couples in similar situations — it appears that there is a pronounced tendency to feel nostalgic about the past and daydream about (a) returning to the earlier marriage (from which, of course, the fatal flaws have been miraculously removed), and (b) having at the very least an illicit relationship with the previous partner, who *is*, of course, the person's *real* wife/husband.

However peculiar this may seem at first glance, you have to remember that Time really *is* a potent healer, and that it is quite natural to remember the 'good bits' of an earlier phase in your life and forget all about the distressing periods. That is one of the reasons why many people really believe that 'school days are the happiest days of your life', that summer weather nowadays is not a patch on the summers of days gone by, etc.

It is a human tendency — normally a very useful one, for it protects us from too many painful recollections — to remember the sunshine, love and laughter of the past, and to forget the cold, wintry days, the resentment and dislike, the loneliness and tears.

Some divorces seem a merciful release to those concerned; to others, they represent a worse experience than bereavement, for death can be an easier fact with which to come to terms eventually, than the loss of a loved one who is still tantalizingly alive.

Excessive dwelling upon the past, however, can never bring it back, and can only antagonize our chances of happiness in the present and the future. Many potentially happy second and subsequent marriages have gone astray because of one or other partner's inability to 'let go'. This is an adjustment that should be made, before another marriage is contemplated.

3.
SEEKING ADVICE

Many tragedies have an isolating effect upon those who suffer them. Bereavement, for instance, can cause an almost hallucinatory sensation of detachment and unreality, and although friends may stay away for a while because they feel tongue-tied in the presence of deep grief, there are usually relatives around to provide a human communication link. Inevitable, too, are the tasks which demand your attention and compliance, such as contacting an undertaker, informing your minister, and communicating with the deceased's solicitor.

Since you are understandably too shocked and upset in this situation to function efficiently, you are obliged to ask how exactly to proceed with matters relating to death, and how to go about the business of arranging for a burial. Such information is nearly always readily forthcoming, for while friends and acquaintances may not know how best to ease your immediate grief, requests for advice and practical help provide them with something definite to do, and an acceptable way of communicating with you without embarrassment.

Faced with a marital collapse, however, or the prospect of the likely demise of your marriage, you may well feel that you are up against a blank wall of silent conspiracy, so difficult does it seem to find a sympathetic yet disinterested listener capable of giving intelligent, practical advice. It seems, sometimes, that friends and relations simply do not want to know — or want to know for the wrong reason of having something new to scandalize about.

You *need* help, however. Following a major row in which divorce threats have been hurled to and fro, the basic security of both partners is at stake — and this can appear as cataclysmic at the time to the instigator of the quarrel as it does to his or her partner. It does not matter one bit, in this instance, whether you are as guilty as hell or as blameless as a newborn babe; primitive instincts are aroused from deep within when 'home' and 'family' are endangered, and there is a need, like that of an injured wild animal, to slink away and lick your wounds. And it helps a great deal to feel that *someone* out there actually cares.

The same situation arises if your marriage is going through a difficult patch and you need advice. Parents who care about you, and your best friends, are automatically inclined to take your side, and while this can be very gratifying in some circumstances it is amazingly irritating when you secretly want to be told that your partner is in the right and that the blame for the rift rests on your shoulders. (This tends to occur when the silent voice of reason inside you keeps protesting at the shabby treatment you have been receiving of late, while the conflicting voice of emotion insists on reminding you that you love your partner deeply.)

The other precarious marital situation in which you desperately need the freedom and opportunity to air your views, is when you are faced with the necessity for making a major decision. You may feel that a separation is essential, and want to be quite sure how to put this over to your unsuspecting husband or wife. You may be sick with the shock of sudden discovery, having just learned that your loving husband or wife is having a passionate affair with someone else. Or you may know instinctively that nothing can save your marriage from disaster, but need to decide how to go about the extremely distasteful job of initiating its dissolution.

Whatever the nature of your need, immediate action is called for. But where can you be sure of finding a friendly, impartial listener capable of giving skilled and practical advice? Here are some suggestions to help you to overcome this problem.

Marriage Guidance Counselling

At one time, the image of marriage guidance counselling was not such that those most in need of it would be inclined to pursue it. The typical counsellor of popular imagination was starchy (and tweedy), moralistic and totally against such notions as abortion, free love, homosexual relationships, pornography and masturbation. To such a person topics like these would be shocking and unworthy of discussion, and most of the advice given out conformed to the adjuncts of the Church and State. Those whom God had joined, let no man indeed dare to part asunder, and marriage was a sufficiently fixed institution to withstand any type of a blow.

Whether or not the first marriage guidance counsellors did conform to this image, is difficult to say. But they certainly do not conform to it now.

I asked Jane, who is a graduate in Social Studies and a trained counsellor, what kind of problems are dealt with today and how those seeking counselling tend to react to the advice they are given. 'We deal with every problem under the sun,' was her reply.

> People come for advice about marriage, divorce, permanent relationships, sexual difficulties, family disputes, arranged marriages, sexual gender — practically anything you can think of and a few you wouldn't dream of, very probably.
>
> Gay people, for instance, maybe new to a big city or perhaps still at school and living at home, come and ask for our help. This is not really our field although we do give them the benefit of our advice if we can — and we always refer them if they ask us to, to advice bureaux specializing in their particular problems.
>
> Also, now people are becoming more aware of us as friendly, non-moralizing individuals, human enough to have experienced a problem or two in our own lives, they are much more inclined to come clean with their query and not beat about the bush. Word is also getting around, as we want it to, that we are perfectly willing to see a husband or wife alone if their partner is unwilling or unable to accompany them; and we also see unmarried people involved in problematical relationships.

And there is no hint of a starchy, old-fashioned image either. Jane was twenty-six, and trendily dressed in a green velvet catsuit, while two other counsellors I met, Roddy and Ann, were both in their thirties and dressed in bright, fashionable clothes. 'We do not try to "keep people married at all costs", especially when they are clearly incompatible with their partners,' they assured me.

> And neither do we throw the Bible at them. We'll certainly recommend a minister for someone to talk to, if they express the need. But by and large, we let our clients, or customers, talk freely about their problems, no holds barred — and then give them the benefit of the most suitable advice we have to offer. They mostly tend to take it, too!

Marriage guidance counselling can be obtained by telephoning for an appointment. The numbers of local offices are listed in the regional telephone directories.

I would emphasize that it *is* preferable to seek counselling together with your partner if you can possibly persuade him or her to accompany you. But, if a great deal of resistance is offered, don't try to force the issue. Explain that *you* want advice, simply because you care enough about the relationship to try to set matters to right. Go on your own if you really want to. At least it is proof positive that you are willing to make an effort. And you will have a skilled listener with whom to talk things over.

Sexual Dysfunction Clinics

A recent survey into the success of sexual problem solving at clinics of marital sexual dysfunction, indicated that a mere nine per cent of those seeking help benefited significantly from the therapy offered. I was very surprised to read this, as the experience most of our patients have of this type of counselling would suggest a far higher success rate.

Basically, couples are accepted for therapy, and are seen together on the first occasion and on the fourth and subsequent ones; the second and third visits are taken up with talking to each partner alone in turn, although both are welcome to come along to the Clinic regardless of whose turn it is to be seen.

The therapists do not insist that the couples are married,

provided they are regular sexual partners. Generally, two therapists are involved in helping each couple and are always present together; trainees may sit and listen and take notes — with the prior consent of the couple.

It is quite usual for those seeking advice to feel acutely embarrassed and even belligerent when faced with the task of discussing their personal sexual difficulties. Impotence, frigidity and premature ejaculation cause a great deal of misery to those affected by them; and this is a fact of which the therapists remain ever aware. Those therapists I have met, and watched at work, are skilled in the arts of tact, discretion, and making their patients, or clients, feel at ease. The shyness most people feel is dispelled by general discussion of the range of topics about which the therapists are consulted, and anxiety diminishes visibly when people realize that their problem is both a common one and capable of resolution.

Anxiety is at the root of the majority of common sexual difficulties, and the clients are taught how to approach sexual sharing in a simple and non-frightening manner. Certain exercises are set each week for the couple to practise at home; and they are made to feel successful and more self-confident as their early efforts are rewarded.

Sex therapists tend, on the whole, to be well-educated, highly trained, sensitive and perceptive people who care a great deal about their work and how their clients feel at different stages of their treatment. If your particular problem is a sexual one, do not hesitate to attend a Sexual Dysfunction Clinic, the address and telephone number of which can generally be supplied by your local Marriage Guidance Counselling headquarters.

There are some things that Sexual Dysfunction Clinics cannot do for you. These are, for the most part, fairly obvious — but the therapists are often requested to solve problems that do not come into their domain, so it is worth mentioning them in passing. First, they cannot advise gay people about their sexual problems, even when these occur within the context of a settled and permanent relationship. In common with Marriage Guidance Counsellors, these therapists refer gay people with problems to centres such as Gay Switchboard, where they can be put in touch with appropriate experts.

Second, they cannot act in the capacity of matchmakers! I was told at the Clinic I visited, that a number of couples book in for treatment in the hopes that if therapy does not work, they will be paired up with compatible sexual partners. In no way do the therapists act in the capacity of a dateline service, so do not look to them if you have a little light relief from present turmoil in mind!

Last, sexual dysfunction therapists cannot wave magic wands and improve a sexual problem which is genetic or hormonal in origin. It is relatively rare for a common problem, such as impotence, to be due to a glandular disorder — in over ninety per cent of cases the problem is what is called 'functional' in origin, meaning that there is no organic basis for the problem which stems, in fact, from a psychological factor such as stress, anxiety, lack of self-confidence, or a deep-rooted fear of the sexual act itself because of some childhood experience.

When sexual dysfunction *is* due to a hormone deficiency, the person to see is a consultant endocrinologist (who specializes in glandular problems), not a therapist whose skill resides in his ability to teach people to eliminate stress factors, anxiety and irrational fears.

Church Ministers

Distressed people who choose to visit a minister in order to discuss a life crisis usually belong to a particular denomination and find it easy to get in touch with the appropriate person. Occasionally, though, my husband and I are requested in the course of our counselling clinics, to suggest a Church minister willing to discuss and advise people upon emotional problems, so a word or two about what ministers have to offer, are appropriate here.

If you are of no particular religious persuasion, visiting a minister may not occur to you. But ministers nowadays tend to be a good deal more approachable and down-to-earth than they were a decade or so ago, and they generally make excellent listeners. I suggested to a Roman Catholic priest one day, who was especially talented in this direction, that his skill probably arose from the frequency with which he listened to Confessions! I was joking but he nodded in agreement. 'No-one, but no-one, would ever feel the remotest compunction about talking over personal problems with a Catholic priest,' he assured me, 'if they had any idea of some of the things we hear in the confessional box over the course of a month!'

The only drawback with Roman Catholic ministers in the present context, however, is that their Church does not permit divorce, and so the advice they give is bound to tend towards keeping couples together rather than advising them to part — although of course a priest may suggest permanent separation as a last resort when a couple is obviously highly incompatible.

It is best to choose a minister whose religious adherence closely parallels your own belief, or you may well end up more confused than you were in the first place. But if religious belief does not enter into the subject and you want a reliable, sympathetic audience, then by all means opt for a visit to the vicarage or presbytery. Generally, a preliminary telephone call asking when visitors are offered appointments is a good idea.

Parents
I could, but will not, write thousands of words upon the wisdom, or otherwise, of bringing parents into marital problems. Everything depends upon your relationship with them, and whether they are able to take the necessarily objective view of the situation, while at the same time extending their love and sympathy to you.

It is usually (although not always) one's mother to whom one turns if one does decide to involve one's parents in a looming divorce — so for convenience's sake I will use the title 'Mother' as representative of either parent. If your relationship with her is ideal, that is you are both loving and close, but recognize that the umbilical cord has definitely been severed, then she may be the very best person to advise you. She will be experienced in the trials, tribulations and joys of married life — and if you need to be told that you are behaving like a stupid, spoiled brat, she is the best qualified person to pass such a verdict. Such a Mother (close indeed to the ideal parent), will be sure to know her son- or daughter-in-law well — and be in a better position than any highly trained counsellor to interpret the nuances of your particular relationship and advise you accordingly.

Never forget that the advice any counsellor, including your

doctor, can give you, is at best general in nature — in much the same way that an astrological forecast for, say, everyone in the western hemisphere born at a particular moment on 25 October 1943, would also be general.

Accuracy and precision enter the astrological forecast picture when the exact place of birth of an individual is taken into account, and the whole series of trends interpreted in the light of present environment, genetic inheritance, and the modifying effects of inborn natural tendencies.

This is the manner in which an intelligent parent is able to score over and over again, when compared to a trained counsellor who often hears one side of a story only and is in no position to make individually directed judgements. These very advantages, on the other hand, can prove potentially damaging to a Mother who is irrevocably biased in favour of her offspring. And to the child who seeks her advice.

There is no lasting satisfaction, really, in being smothered with love and sympathy, when what one really requires is an objective opinion as well as a good listener. If you know deep down that you are bound to be right in the eyes of your idolizing parent, while your actual need is for practical advice, then do the courageous thing and avoid flying to the outstretched parental arms.

Many parents, particularly those of only children, are incapable of recognizing that their child is an adult, and — even though sometimes not consciously aware of it — do everything within their power to reinstate their 'baby' back safely at home with them, where they can be looked after and protected from upsetting (and disloyal) relationships with other people. Such parents really are the very last people on earth to recognize this subversive tendency — and in most cases are, paradoxically, so genuinely concerned with their child's welfare that, if they understood their own ulterior motives in encouraging a son or daughter to leave a troubled marital relationship, they would immediately step aside from the issue. The tragedy is that they are at a conscious level, motivated by the very best of intentions when they suggest 'coming home to think things over', 'giving one's partner a piece of one's mind', and so on.

But the fact remains that an overattached parent can severely worsen a troubled marital partnership by his or her natural partisanship.

Best Friends
Most of us who are blessed with true best friends know their value and have not the faintest hesitation in consulting them about marital problems. Doing so generally provides enormous relief, and in no way precludes our also seeking some professional advice about, say, sexual difficulties, severe incompatibility of temperament etc.

The 'best friends' to be wary of, though, are recently acquired and untested ones whose real allegiance is a little unclear. Many single people, as well as married couples, run from the scene as from the plague itself, when marital disharmony rears its ugly head and sympathy and help are required. One feels sadly let down — and almost sufficiently ostracized to feel convinced that one has a serious and contagious disease rather than the need to discuss marital strife.

Under these circumstances, the safest advice is secretly to demote such self-professed 'best friends' to the rank of passable but unreliable acquaintances, and promise oneself two important things forthwith. One is to make the effort to form lasting friendships with individuals of either sex who really deserve the title of 'friend' and who are capable of loyalty. The other is to seek specialist help from one of the sources I have already mentioned, in order to make certain that your need for understanding and help is properly satisfied.

4.

REACHING A DECISION

Once you have obtained all the advice you need, and feel satisfied that it is the best available — how do you go about putting it into practice?

This may seem self-evident. But the fact remains that, however many people you turn to for help, the final decision, and the freedom to act, lie with you alone. This is as it should be. No-one should presume to dictate a particular plan of campaign to you as though it were the only valid opinion in existence — and you should beware of anyone who attempts to do so, except in the most extreme circumstances.

I am referring, when I say this, to a situation in which your life or the life of your children, is endangered by a violent partner. Or one in which your marriage has become so intolerable to you, that your mental and physical health are in imminent danger of collapse. Then you need — if indeed you entertain any doubts yourself — to be told categorically to get out, and to get out fast, even though this may possibly prove a temporary measure.

There is one type of advice about which you should be very wary — and that is the unsolicited variety. Of course it can happen that parents, family or close friends worry about your welfare, and feel that they can see potential dangers in a marriage or relationship of which you are unaware. By all means hear them out, and promise to think about what they have said. Actually *do* so, too, for it is perfectly possible that the points they have raised are valid and worthy of consideration. But refuse to be swayed by the opinion of others, if you are convinced deep inside that you know better.

Few people who have plumbed the depths of a passionate relationship would deny that love is frequently, if not exactly blind, then at least fearfully myopic. The man or woman for whom you have fallen so heavily, may well be completely unsuitable as a permanent partner whatever your feelings to the contrary. So try to assess the situation objectively from time to time in the light of other peoples' opinion, however resentful you may feel when they advise you to break up your relationship forthwith.

Just remember, however, that they are as capable of forming false impressions as you yourself are — and in the final reckoning always obey your own inner convictions.

The best advice in the world, though, however impelled you are to follow it, can present practical problems in the demands it makes on your courage, tolerance and pride. So, before we consider how to go about matters when separation or divorce are inevitable, it is worth taking a look at advice typically given to combat the various 'divorce factors' I dealt with in Chapter Two.

Teenage Marriage
In this particular circumstance I feel that I am writing for two very different categories of reader. The first consists of teenagers who are debating an early wedding or who are already getting into marital difficulties, and the second includes the worried parents of these two groups.

If you are in the sixteen- to eighteen-year-old age group, deeply in love, and frustrated beyond measure at the negative attitude of your parents and other relatives, you may well have already sworn that you are going to get married as soon as you possibly can, regardless of opposition. There is something nobly defiant about the apparent courage of this decision which puts one in mind of the attitude of Arthur Wellesley, Duke of Wellington who, when faced with opposition, criticism and scandal, cried 'Publish and be damned,' and went ahead and did what he wanted to do, regardless.

Notice, though, that I referred to the 'apparent' courage of the decision to go ahead and get married, ignoring all advice to the contrary. However passionately you may be in love with one another at the moment, just think of how you could possibly feel if plagued by domestic stresses, a shortage of cash and no job prospects in a year or so's time. You probably feel that your love is sufficiently deep and enduring to withstand such a test — and if so, draw upon its strength and ask yourselves the following questions.

'First, with the present divorce rate as high as it is, dispite so many marriages starting off, like ours would, in happiness and harmony — are we prepared to risk our love being destroyed by factors beyond our power to control? Such as the constant need for economy, no cash to spend on entertainment and clothes, pressing debts which we cannot meet?'

'Second, does either of us secretly feel that anything could be gained from a year or two more of youthful freedom before settling down to a permanent relationship? Or, if the dole queue is already an established fact in our life, would it possibly be better for both of us to undergo some sort of training before we marry so that we have something to turn to when the unemployment rate starts noticeably to fall?'

'Third, could we cope with the demands, and supply the needs, of a small baby, were one to arrive before we had planned for it? Remembering that no contraceptive measures are infallible, and there is always the long weekend, late night after a party or other occasion on which the Pill, the sheath or the cap are simply forgotten about.'

If you still feel that you should go ahead, take the following precautionary measure against future misunderstandings. Agree together on a list of all the possible problems which might threaten your happiness and the permanence of your marriage during its first five years (which are usually said to be the hardest, anyway); consult the appropriate section in Chapter Two, and add any others I may not have mentioned. Then spend an evening apart in your separate homes, writing down how you feel you would react under the circumstances to each of them, and what you would suggest as possible solutions.

Compare notes the next time you meet, and while you can safely congratulate yourselves on all the points upon which you agree, be especially on the look-out for points of variance. Discuss these fully, instead of sweeping them under the carpet with a shrug on the assumption that they 'won't happen, anyway!' They often do, which is why so many marriages come to grief. And there is perhaps no other circumstance in which it is truer to say, that forewarned is forearmed.

If you are already married and are regretting it, think several times before you succumb to the temptation of packing your bags and returning home to your parents. If you are fighting a great deal, perhaps violently, it may be an idea to spend a night or two with a close friend of the same sex as yourself — to avoid adding recriminations of infidelity to the problem. This will give you a breathing space in which you can think things over and obtain any help you may need.

But do not even consider making the separation permanent, until you and your partner have got together again, once tempers have cooled, for a reasonable discussion. The younger you are, the more emotional resilience you are likely to have — and the less deep-rooted cynicism. Try again — and again — before you are prepared to admit that your marriage is a failure.

If you are a parent, worried out of your mind by a teenage son or daughter who is determined to marry at a tender age, regardless of any arguments you can produce against the idea, here are a few things which you should avoid doing at all costs. First, do not tell your child that he or she *owes* it to *you*, not to ruin their life and your happiness by getting married before they are sufficiently mature.

Second, do not weep, scream, wring your hands, threaten to 'have it out' with the parents or guardian of your child's prospective partner; or, to put it rather more bluntly, behave as immaturely as you feel *they* are behaving.

Third, do not throw them out of the house if they refuse to change their mind. You are only responsible for their happiness and welfare up to a certain point — and if they insist on pursuing a course of action you are convinced will make them unhappy, then they must go ahead and do so. This may sound hard and unfeeling, but it is far less hard than banking on being able to influence them as you would wish, and forbidding them to darken your doorstep again if you fail in your attempt. After all, you have your own happiness and that of your wife or husband to consider, too — and without any shadow of a doubt, great misery for all concerned would result from severing relationships with your child in a fit of anger and emotional pain. Better to try a reasoned approach when discussing the matter, pointing out how *they* rather than you, may very well get badly hurt by their marrying too young. If you do not succeed in your objective, try not to feel too badly about it and give in gracefully. Refusal to row is far more likely to influence their ultimate decision favourably than hurling abuse at them. So whatever you do — remain friendly.

If your child is already unhappily married, try to be a superb listener to his or her woes without dictating the course of action you feel should be followed. And try not to criticize your son- or daughter-in-law too strongly, how ever much you may feel inclined to do so. If your child is being physically assaulted or seems on the verge of a breakdown — then by all means offer them the opportunity of returning home to you, forthwith.

If a series of minor tiffs are the cause of the problem, though, and a more serious tiff than usual brings your offspring to your doorstep, bags packed and ready to find a solicitor — give them a cup of coffee and a sympathetic talking to, and (if they are short of cash), the fare home! All marriages have their difficulties and need to be worked at, and you are perfectly within your rights to remind them of this fact!

Redundancy and Unemployment
We looked at the strains which redundancy and unemployment can place on a relationship. Advice on how to diminish these strains is difficult to put into practice all the time the situation remains unaltered — for while many types of harmful stress can be dealt with successfully, unemployment presents problems which are not immediately capable of solution.

All that can reasonably be recommended, is that you *refuse* to become too downhearted by repeated failures to obtain the job you want, and take *any* kind of work of which you are capable. Unemployment is not your fault, but your morale may suffer badly if you feel you are letting your partner and family down. And, as we have seen, violent rows born of anger and guilt can result.

Other types of work pressure can cause strained marital relationships, and it is possible to diminish these to a certain extent — as you would certainly be advised to do, if you attended for marriage counselling. The pressure I mean is the exact opposite of unemployment, and is brought about by work that is *too* demanding of one's time and energy if one is married and wishes to enjoy one's domestic and social life.

Everyone reading this book would doubtless be able to think of at least one example of a marriage that has been either seriously threatened, if not wrecked, by the overlong working hours of one or other partner. And nowadays, this is just as likely to apply to the wife as to the husband. I always think marriages that fail because those concerned strive *too* hard to make money, are particularly tragic.

Michael Savage was a case in point, and someone I knew personally as opposed to someone who came to us for counselling. He was thirty-six when I first met him, and a successful and popular surgeon at the hospital where I did my training. He was, at that time, a Senior Registrar in both general and arterial surgery, with a full operating list and ward round to complete every week day, as well as medical students to teach and a time-consuming research project to complete.

He was married, had two children aged six and eight, and worked all the hours that God sent. I knew he was devoted to his wife and family, as he often used to bemoan the little time that he was able to spend with them as well as the fact that, since he was so often called out to surgical emergencies in the middle of the night, he was perpetually tired and slept most of the time when he *did* have a weekend off.

Michael's research project was aimed at producing a thesis for the post-graduate degree of Mastership of Surgery, which would, he knew, place him in excellent stead for a Consultant post at the teaching hospital when one became available. So he went without a summer holiday for three years running, spent as much off-duty time as he could in the laboratory, and many hours between times, studying in the library.

Not easy to obtain at the best of times, his first attempt at the Master's degree failed, and he was obliged to spend even longer hours away from home. Tragically, he learned that his second attempt to obtain it had been successful the day after his wife told him that she could endure a lonely life no longer — and was leaving him for his best friend.

With today's high cost of living, of course, it is extremely tempting to make as much money as possible. There is no doubt, either, that a good, private education is a priceless gift from which your child or children can benefit for the rest of their lives. But this takes a great deal of self-sacrifice, as does earning sufficient money to pay for expensive presents, a new car and holidays abroad.

To avoid the pitfall of your marriage slowly coming adrift in your absence as you strive to earn as much as you possibly can, discuss priorities with your partner before the dangers arise. And determine on a mutually satisfactory lifestyle *before* you apply for a highly competitive job which may dominate your waking and sleeping hours for years to come.

Physical and Mental Illness

If your problem is chronic illness affecting either you, your partner, your child or an elderly relative who lives with you, you may be so tired — and so busy — that you haven't the time to ask for advice, and certainly could not contemplate altering your lifestyle. Meanwhile, you may be sadly aware that your marriage is under a severe strain, but feel quite unable to do anything about it.

Your main problem, in fact, is *not* so much the forbidding task of combining the role of full-time nurse with that of wife or husband and parent, as it is the understandable difficulty of seeing the wood for the trees. And by this I mean taking a detached and realistic look at the problems as a whole, both in terms of your patient's real needs, the possible availability of outside help, and the extent to which other family members, including yourself, are affected by your nursing duties.

If you are frequently tearful with exhaustion, have no interest in, or indeed time for, sex, and feel anger, resentment and guilt as a result — the chances are that you and others are suffering just as much as the invalid. Make sure, therefore, that you have explored every avenue of available help and be prepared to delegate some of your nursing duties, either to a part-time nurse, another family member or even a day care or residential centre.

This suggestion scandalizes some people who feel it entirely wrong to allow 'strangers' or even another relative to take over for a time, especially when the patient is an elderly parent, a child or a husband or wife. But, if all the joy of life for you has been effectively obscured by the dark mists of fatigue, worry and perpetual work, the time has come to call a halt.

Suppose you have several children, one of whom is severely retarded and has spina bifida into the bargain; with the result that the child can do nothing to help him or herself and is probably incontinent. Or suppose that you look after your elderly father, who has become senile of late, and often wanders about at night, wetting himself and becoming obstructive when you offer to help. Or perhaps your wife or husband has a chronic sickness, such as multiple sclerosis, Parkinson's disease or the effects of a stroke? Or a serious mental illness which prevents him or her from working?

Whatever the particular circumstances, remember that it can sometimes be in the interest of the family as a whole, to seek hospitalization for the patient — either for a time, to enable you to rest, recreate and generally recover from chronic tiredness, or on a permanent basis. It is very much a matter of individual viewpoint, whether you would allow your marital partner to go permanently into a home or hospital ward — my own is that one's paramount duty is to love and succour one's mate, first and foremost, and that this is more important than anything else could be. By this token, I would steel myself to bear the pain of sending an elderly parent or defective child into a home, if I were unable to afford suitable accommodation and the necessary equipment for them at home, as well as professional part-time nursing care.

Whatever your decision, just remember the cruel though indisputable fact, that a person devoid of the powers of reason and of analytical thought, is incapable of 'thinking the situation through' and of reaching the conclusion that you are harsh, unfeeling and failing in your duty to them. And you can torture yourself quite unnecessarily with the mistaken idea of your own unkindness.

My advice would be to follow the whole of the marriage vow — including the words 'in sickness and in health' — and to put the good of your partner as your top priority. The hardest decision to make is when this good conflicts with the good of your children, and this is a choice about which no-one who does not know you intimately is in a position to advise you.

Alcohol and Drug Dependence
The same applies when alcohol or drugs constitute the health threat. By all means search every avenue for a possible cure, and give unstintingly all the love and support you have to give. Prevent communications from breaking down by pointing out to your partner that his health and his self-respect are being ruined — and plead with him, time and time again to stop. But only you, however, can decide whether you are prepared to let your life be ruined by the tragedy of your partner's addiction; and if not, where to draw the line.

Infidelity
As I pointed out earlier, the best way to cope with your own infidelity is to resolve never to be unfaithful again — and to defuse your inner anxiety and guilt by discussing the problem with either a professional counsellor or a friend you know you can trust. This advice applies to the kind of person I described, who slips up 'once only' — and is deeply distressed by self-blame and guilt.

For if you belong in the other category I described, and make a habit of sleeping around, either you and your partner have already agreed to run your marriage along these lines, or you are heading deliberately towards the nearest Divorce Court. Either way round, overwhelming guilt is unlikely to be your problem.

What should you do if you suddenly discover that your husband or wife is having — or has just had — an affair, either because he or she has confessed as much to you or because someone else has made it their business to inform you of the fact?

There is all the difference in the world between 'having an affair' and 'having just had one'. If you and your partner have always been very close it is bad enough to learn the latter, and can be intolerable to be told the former. Whatever you do, though, resist the temptation to pack your bags and leave on the spot — unless of course to remain at home is likely only to worsen matters.

If your husband or wife is genuinely and deeply sorry, prepared to sever all relations with his or her illicit lover, and clearly in need of your understanding and forgiveness — make a superhuman effort to offer these freely. But do have a long discussion about the matter first, both of you putting forward your own views on why the affair occurred and how a recurrence can be avoided at all costs.

Never be afraid to say how deeply hurt you feel, and how your trust has been betrayed — after all, you *do* and it *has*, and you must be allowed to express your feelings of anger and pain as they affect you. But don't nag, complain and weep for hours, as this can evoke both resentment and rebellion if carried to too great a length. A frank discussion may, on the other hand, result in greater understanding and closeness than had existed previously.

If, however, you confront your loved one with your awareness that he or she is having an affair with someone else — or alternatively, he or she tells you so, without promising to break off the relationship — you are faced with a different problem altogether. If you love your partner very much, and feel that with a little outside help, or even independently, you can weather the storm, well and good. But if your world seems to be disintegrating around you and you cannot cope, then you may well be right in feeling that the tactic of mental cruelty is being employed and that the only answer, if you are to regain your peace of mind, is separation and possibly divorce.

Divergence of Interests
You can avoid waking up one morning three months after you get married and realizing that you and your new partner have nothing in common, by being as perceptive — and honest — as possible during the early days of your courtship. If you do as Bernard did during his engagement to Molly (see page 30), and go along with the other person's wishes and beliefs every time, then you may well experience similar doubts as to your suitability.

It is simple to avoid this dilemma, however, by agreeing from the start to 'share as well as care', and swop opinions, ideas, tastes and hobbies as widely as money and time allow. Even if you cannot for the moment indulge your passion for surfing/horse riding/Go Kart racing, due to lack of facilities — and your fiancé is unable to hang-glide/orienteer/go ballroom dancing because he is studying for exams — you should each make your enthusiasm for these activities perfectly clear to one another. In that way you are likely to grow closer together rather than farther apart — and develop a wide range of new interests into the bargain. Be prepared to dispose with old prejudices, though; if you are dead against broadening your horizons and do not want to share, then you should ask yourself whether you really want to get married at all.

When I advise being as perceptive as possible, I mean keeping a critical — if loving — eye upon the differences as well as the similarities between your daily lifestyles, attitudes to the earning and the spending of money, moral and religious beliefs, and your feelings about whether to have children or not. Whatever you do, avoid agreeing or pretending to agree with a view that is at a total variance to your inmost convictions.

One of the most exciting opportunities that marriage affords, that of exploring the depths of one another's mind and heart, can become instead a bloody battle field of mutual destruction, if you are too lazy or too scared to examine the grounds for future antagonism before it is too late. This is not to say that people cannot have opposing views on all manner of subjects, yet be very happily married.

Differences of opinion are only destructive where early deceit has indicated agreement in the place of dissent — or in the relatively rare cases where strongly varying religious convictions preclude the possibility of an harmonious union.

Sexual Problems
Obtaining professional, skilled help for troublesome problems is always a good idea and, as we have seen, the best place to ask for advice regarding sexual difficulties is at a marital Sexual Dysfunction Clinic.

This is fine, you may say feelingly, but how do I persuade my husband/wife/lover to accompany me to such a place, when he/she has such a hang-up about their problem that they will barely discuss it with me — let alone a couple of strangers?

I can only advise you to persist in your attempts to get your partner to go along with you one evening, and see how they feel about it. Point out that there is no constraint upon them ever to attend for another session if they dislike it as much as they imagine they will — at least (you can say), they will have showed willing. And it may help if you point out that the problem, if simple, more than likely has an equally simple remedy. If complex — then there is all the more need for skilled help.

Try not to get too worked up by their refusal, and determine to try again on another occasion. Normally I would say that it is better not to try to persuade people to do something against their will — but there is rather a sense of urgency in cases of sexual problems, for they can very quickly both take a strong root *and* lead to destructively bitter quarrels.

Here are some details of two couples who attended Sexual Dysfunction Clinics, and of the advice they were given there. The first is a story of unqualified success.

Bob and Margot, both in their thirties, came to see me because Bob was suffering from impotence. That was the problem in a nutshell, but it took a visit from Margot alone, followed by a half-hour interview with the pair of them to discover what precisely was troubling them.

Bob gave a terse description of his malady. 'Everything was OK until about six weeks ago,' he assured me.

> Then, as you probably remember, Mother passed away and straight after the funeral I started to work very late hours in connection with an important projected pitch by the advertising company I work for.
>
> Then Ted, our ten-year-old, fell about sixteen feet out of a tree he had climbed, and went through the greenhouse roof of our next door neighbour — who dislikes kiddies at the best of times!
>
> Not only was Ted concussed and badly cut — but he remained unconscious in the hospital for over an hour and a half, and Margot, who as you know is four months pregnant, nearly started to miscarry, she was so distressed about him. To cap it all, Mr Biggs next door has threatened to sue for trespass, although I've already paid generous compensation for the damage to his greenhouse!

It seemed that since the beginning of this particularly stressful time, Bob had been experiencing weaker and weaker erections, and in the end had been unable to obtain one at all. I put both of their minds at rest, by assuring them that acute worry and stress can have just the effects he had been noticing — but referred them both to the Sexual Dysfunction Clinic anyway.

I saw them three months later about a different matter — and they both looked a great deal more relaxed.

'The trouble we consulted you about last time, has entirely disappeared,' Bob told me, smiling.

> The therapists at the clinic really put you at your ease, and they gave us a simple routine to work to, in our own good time at home. Three times a week, we had to massage one another naked on a mattress on the floor — but intercourse was forbidden, and at first we weren't even allowed to stimulate each other.
>
> I found my erections returning some considerable time before we were allowed to make love — in fact I got quite frustrated! And we are welcome to go back any time we want to — for a chat, or further advice or help if we need it.

The same basic routine is suggested, with minor variations, for most of the people who attend with sexual disturbances — and counselling given for whatever emotional problems are involved. Harriet and Conrad, who were in their thirties and forties respectively, came complaining of Harriet's lack of sexual interest, and of Conrad's failure to maintain an erection. They were very tense when they came to see me, and Harriet spoke for both of them. In fact they did not exchange a single word with one another all the time they were in the surgery — which made me wonder whether Conrad was attending out of constraint only.

I referred them to the Clinic, and heard about them only indirectly from one of the therapists. Naturally anything revealed by patients is in strictest confidence — but by the time I met the therapist Harriet and Conrad had emigrated to New Zealand, and there seemed no prospect of their returning for years.

'They were difficult people to deal with,' the therapist, Sam, admitted. 'Time and again they returned to see us, without having followed our suggested routine at all. They even attempted intercourse before they were meant to — and complained that they experienced the same trouble as before!'

Nevertheless it transpired that success had been achieved at last, and a threatened divorce averted by the reinstitution of enjoyable love-making. Which was well worth the effort — although they attended for a total of five months before they achieved their objective.

Physical and Mental Cruelty
These two forms of behaviour are hard to define — and only indisputably present for all the world to see when their effects on the victim are extreme. As I said before, the infliction of most marital cruelty is a peculiarly personal thing, requiring knowledge of the victim's special weaknesses if it is to have maximum effect. But certain kinds are so gross that I never have the slightest hesitation in counselling patients to separate from their spouses immediately, ignoring all pretence of marital duty, lingering love for the oppressor, and so on.

The first of these, physical cruelty, is illustrated by the case history of Brenda, a pleasant lady in her late forties who worked for the Gas Board and lived an ordinary suburban kind of existence just as do millions of people in common with her. Her husband, Norman, was a factory manager, and they were well known to be devoted to one another — and hardly ever separated, apart from when they were at work.

Norman, however, started to show signs of change after his fiftieth birthday, and perplexed Brenda by buying youthful gear, exchanging the sedate family car for a powerful motorbike, and going out several evenings a week without her. Despite her distress, he was very cagey about where he actually went — and always refused her naïve requests to take her with him.

Eventually a friend at work told Brenda that Norman had been seen out in a night club with a tawdry-looking blonde and, despite her feelings of pain and dismay, Brenda spoke to her husband about the story when he arrived home from work. He lost his temper completely, and the one time gentle, peace-loving man picked up a leather belt he often wore and gave her a sound thrashing.

Practically in a state of collapse, Brenda staggered next door to her nearest neighbour, where she spent the night. She returned home the next morning — and found a note from her husband, who had left for work, saying that he never wished to converse with her again, but that he had no intention of leaving home, so she would just have to tolerate the situation.

She discovered that from then onwards, his behaviour was absolutely predictable. If she kept silent, cooked his meals, washed his clothes and kept the place tidy — peace, indeed total silence, reigned. If she as much as opened her mouth to ask Norman the simplest domestic question, let alone question him about his activities, he gave her a good hiding. She was sure he was mentally sick, but obviously was in no position to persuade him of the fact.

When she finally sought my advice, she had lost two and a half stone in weight, was suffering from severe sleeplessness, and had had two ribs fractured, multiple bruises and frequent black eyes. I told her to leave home immediately — to pack a suitcase while her husband was at work, and leave a brief note saying that she was suing for divorce. This she did — with no real persuasion on my part — and as Norman was picked up by the police for assault about a month later, and found to be suffering from acute paranoid schizophrenia, I think Brenda was lucky to escape with her life and sanity intact.

Mental cruelty is hard to define — and can be difficult to prove if you try to use it as your plea when suing for divorce. You may know very well that a particular approach is mentally cruel, and recognize when it is being used in attack against you *and* when you are guilty of using it yourself against your partner.

It may sound trivial in Court to claim that your partner is being mentally cruel to you by playing his radio day and night — but he may very well be, if he knows that you are unable to stomach pop music at any price, yet persists in playing it round the clock, and turned up to full volume.

By the same token, in order to punish your husband for an offence you may well decide to give him fillet steak every evening for a week, knowing full well that he is a purist vegan. Yet cooking steak for one's spouse can be admitted to with wide-eyed innocence to the accompaniment of protestations of having only his best interests at heart — which is very sneaky, to say the least.

In fact so evil a practice do I consider the infliction of

deliberate mental cruelty that I would advise any sufferer to depart forthwith, unless the partner can be persuaded to cease his or her game immediately.

Reluctant Parenthood

If your lack of domestic skill and inability to cope with a demanding baby are posing a bad strain upon your marriage, you are (although you are unlikely to think so!) in a rather more fortunate category than many other folk facing marital problems. This is because a lack of skill and knowledge are relatively easy to remedy compared, say, to coping with a partner's infidelity, a recurrent sexual problem or the stresses and strains of a busy job.

Of course, part of your problem may very well be related to *your* demanding work schedule. If you have a young baby to cope with, housework that appears to reproduce itself a thousand times over regardless of how hard you try, and a job that insists on the maintenance of a high standard, then how the deuce (you ask) are you ever to learn how to cope any better?

Do not panic, despair — or, most important — lose your sense of humour. With a home, baby, job and lover or husband to love, you have a great deal of potential for satisfaction and happiness in your life, provided you know how to go about enjoying it. Sit down with your partner when neither of you are speechless with fatigue, and work out a plan by which you can *both* put things to rights, learn basic essential skills both of you presently lack — and acquire a neat and well-organized home into the bargain.

Start by accepting someone's kind offer of a day of baby sitting — and set to on the house, working together, and deciding in advance who will be responsible for which jobs. It is surprising how very much better a grubby, untidy home looks once all the rubbish is rounded up and secured in dustbin bags, the windows have been cleaned, and unnecessary papers, toys and miscellaneous items tidied away into cupboards and drawers.

Hoover the carpets, sweep and wash the kitchen floor, change the sheets and duvet covers, and you are practically there! Give the place a quick dust, have a bath and a snack —

and go and collect your baby from his kind minder, happy that you are bringing him back to a transformed home.

No-one would suggest that you clean the place as thoroughly as this, every day — or even every week. But do work out and *write down* a mutually agreeable time-table you are both willing to keep to — and it is only fair that both partners contribute to the active running of the home, especially with both of you working. Gone, thank heavens, are the days when a man can reasonably expect to be waited on. There is no earthly reason why you should not share the dusting, hoovering, bed-making and financial management of the home — just as you might well enjoy sharing bathing the baby, shopping and washing the car.

And if cooking or child care are particular worries in your life — either get a baby-sitter and go to evening classes together; or get your partner to mind the baby while you go alone; or if there are no suitable classes in your area, buy or borrow a good book on the subject and read it together.

Make a combined effort, learn to laugh at your mistakes, and above all *keep trying* and never be too proud to ask for advice. Any marital problems resulting from your inefficiency should rapidly disappear.

My friend Ruth found herself in this position a year or so after marrying. She was a postgraduate student at a London college, married to the director of a firm of 'head-hunters'. Housework was always a bit of a problem although they had a large, pleasant house with lots of handsome, modern furniture. The arrival of Justine was the last straw — they hadn't the ghost of an idea how to bath, change or feed a baby — and Ruth had no time to learn prior to giving birth, as she was so busy with her studies and social life.

Life looked grim as the dust piled up round Ruth and baby during her postnatal recovery period. Postnatal depression set in — and her husband worried by his wife's condition, the state of the home, and the stresses of his busy job, started to drink too much. He came to me in a state of panic one day, having just been summonsed for drunken driving. I calmed his fears as best I could, went to see Ruth and the baby, and advised them on a number of emergency measures they could take, to prevent the situation from deteriorating further. Ruth attended baby care classes as soon as she was fit to do so — and enjoyed them so much that she decided to write a paper on child care as part of her college course!

At a practical level, the state of the home grew steadily better, and Chris, her husband, had no further temptations with respect to alcohol.

If you are a reluctant parent simply because you did not really want to have — or father — a child in the first place, then you owe it to the child, as well as to each other, to make the very best of the situation you can. For with contraceptives and legalized abortion freely available for all, having the child is very much the result of a conscious choice and not the inevitable outcome of a 'mistake' as it used once to be.

Refusing to Accept the Present

I have already given advice about this tendency, one which should be avoided at all costs if you value the present and the future. If the past seems infinitely dear to you and you feel a profound sense of loss, try to control your thoughts, or at least discuss your problem with a sympathetic friend or counsellor. Do not make the mistake of telling your partner how much you miss the man/woman he or she replaced — a person would need to be superhuman to endure listening and rows are almost inevitable. After all, you probably would object if you had to listen for hours to a wistful account of your lover's or spouse's past. You might even be tempted to invite him/her to try to reclaim it if it was so marvellous.

He or she would only have to be in the mood to take you seriously and follow your advice — and your marriage could be in dangerously deep water overnight. Try tolerance if you *are* treated to blow by blow accounts of a nostalgically remembered previous marriage — and point out kindly the unwisdom of dwelling on the subject. If you are tempted to do this yourself, then don't be surprised if the consequences are unpleasant and unexpected!

5.

ADMITTING MISTAKES AND MAKING THE BREAK

Most of us are scared of being laughed at or criticized, and this fear can be powerful enough to shape the course of our lives in a way that we secretly find intolerable. Some people even get married while entertaining a nagging doubt as to the wisdom of doing so, when they discover towards the end of their engagement that they are less compatible than they had hoped, but are too scared of looking foolish by calling the whole thing off — especially once the Church or Register Office has been booked and the invitations sent out.

It takes a formidable amount of courage to proclaim to the world that you have made a mistake, which is why few weddings are cancelled at the last moment. It is far more tempting to quell your doubts by telling yourself that all you are experiencing is an attack of last-minute nerves, than it is to return the rings, cancel the catering arrangements and agree to part as amicably as possible.

I would urge anyone who consulted me on the matter, to summon up as much courage as they possibly can, and only proceed with *any* major life event if they feel that it is right for them. This is not the same thing as backing out of a plan or agreed course of action solely on the grounds that the thought of it frightens you. Sometimes a healthy appreciation of the dangers, social or otherwise, of a given action can stimulate your 'flight or fright' mechanism into releasing just the right amount of adrenaline into your blood-stream. And you deliver your first public speech, take out your first gall-bladder or take your driving test with confidence, skill and precision.

But when you wake, in the small hours of the morning, to a quiet persistent voice inside which repeats, over and over again, that you are heading for disaster if you do so-and-so — then listen to it! And this applies as much to a forthcoming wedding as it does to any other important event. For when you stop to think of all the people of whose ridicule you are so scared, ask yourself how many of them would actually care a hoot afterwards if you and your partner were miserably incompatible, and would help you through the wretched stages of marital breakdown and divorce.

Never allow fear of any kind to drive you into a marriage you feel less than happy about. And never allow it to keep you tied to a partner to whom — despite repeated attempts to grow together — you are basically unsuited. So far as I can tell, we only have one life — or at least, we only have one life on this planet, under the present conditions of existence. Some ascetics may draw comfort from their certainty that their trials and tribulations in this world merely represent the workings of Karmic law and that things are likely to be a great deal better 'next time round'. But for most of us, this view, while possible to understand at a theoretical level, is impossible to live by. And we owe it to ourselves us to utilize our courage, strength and resilience in the pursuit of a suitable lifestyle.

Divorce is a necessary — in fact, an absolutely essential — evil, in the same way that a major operation is 'evil', and undesirable unless the indisputable need for it arises. When an organ becomes diseased, however, and its continued presence within the body will seriously affect the individual, probably causing its ultimate decease, then the 'maiming' effect of a surgical manoeuvre is transformed into a positive and desirable action to be carried out at the earliest opportunity. Any surgeon will admit that the need for surgery is an admission of failure — both of a bodily organ or system *and* of medicine to discover a cure. But no-one would deny the wisdom of removing an inflamed appendix or a ruptured spleen. And, by that token, few would deny the wisdom of ending a hopeless marriage whose long-term effects could cause hatred, despair and permanent emotional scarring.

Of course getting divorced is an unpleasant process — and few people, in the early days of their love affair, can ever seriously imagine it happening to *them*. It is capable of causing great stress and of plunging its victims into the depths of depression; but never forget that, to a certain extent, you can control its power to harm *you*. One thing it does have to recommend it; at least, like a wretched marriage, it does not go on for ever! It is a lot easier to see, or at least to believe in, the light at the end of the tunnel, when you are in the throes of divorce, than it is when you are married to someone whom you have grown to detest over the years.

People whom I find very difficult to advise, are those who suffer from chronic rather than acute marital problems, which have dragged on for so long that one or other partner — sometimes both — have come almost to disregard them. Just as Time is a great healer, so being constantly subjected to pain in the end dulls the senses and makes the victim a great deal less sensitive. One or other partner hurts his or her spouse so often and so much — that he or she ceases to complain, seeking only to live from one day to the next, and hoping ultimately for a happy release from the situation.

This kind of apathy is a major factor in marriages which amaze the concerned spectator by reason of their continuing existence. I am referring, of course, to marriages which feature physical abuse, gross infidelity, alcoholism or drug dependence among their attributes. What often happens is that the wife — or husband — fails to take action at the onset of the trouble and, growing apathetic, just puts up with a wretched way of life.

Joan and Ray were a couple whose home situation was drawn to my attention indirectly. A note was pushed under the surgery door, asking me to call at the Smith's home to see the small daughter. I assumed one or other parent had written the note, which was unsigned. At my second attempt to gain entry the door of the council house was opened by Mrs Smith, dressed in a filthy dressing gown and with her hair in curlers — and she was clearly amazed to see me.

The little girl *did* in fact have a nasty cold — but was also covered on her back and chest with bruises of all ages and in different stages of development. These, claimed Mrs Smith, were due to Lorraine's habit of falling down stairs so often! She also muttered something about 'nosey neighbours', from which I gathered that the people next door had finally taken matters into their own hands as they obviously suspected, or knew, that child abuse was going on.

I told Mrs Smith outright that I did not believe her story of how her daughter's bruises had come about — at which point the woman burst into tears and collapsed into a chair.

> No, doctor, you are quite right, of course — and I know I should have done something about it all years ago. Ever since Ray started to gamble and drink, he's been coming home three or four evenings a week, and hitting me if I as much as open my mouth to him. And, unfortunately, he cannot bear Lorraine crying. She used to be a happy child, and hardly ever cried — but now she is older and can understand things she gets scared when she hears me being hit, and she screams her head off.
>
> The effect on Ray is to make him even more violent than before — and as soon as he has beaten the hell out of me, he goes into her room and thumps her. I know I should leave him, and take Lorraine with me. But I have a previous conviction for shoplifting and I am so scared that if I tried to get away and start divorce proceedings, neither of us would end up with custody of Lorraine, who might get put into care. Anyway, Ray could never care for himself, and if he started to drink more than he is drinking at the moment — and had an accident — I'd never be able to forgive myself!

Of course people should be encouraged to decide on their own priorities and loyalties — but I quickly pointed out that, faced with a violent husband and a defenceless five-year-old daughter, her duty very definitely lay in protecting her child. To which Mrs Smith soon agreed, particularly when I pointed out the extreme unliklihood of her losing Lorraine 'into care' if she and her husband separated, simply because of a single shoplifting offence which had taken place ten years earlier.

She left her husband and went to stay with her mother, taking Lorraine with her. Ray made several abortive attempts at scaring his wife into returning to him. But once Mrs Smith had taken the bit between her teeth, so to speak, there was no holding her — and the divorce proceedings and custody agreement went through without a hitch.

Six months after it was all over, Joan Smith looked a different woman — as, in many respects, she was. She told me:

> The only thing that vexes me now, is why on earth I let it all go on for as long as I did. Lorraine might have been badly injured or even killed. She is much better now, but she still has nightmares and is still wetting the bed. But I give her lots of love and kisses and a special treat whenever she has a dry night. And I am sure we will get there in the end!

I've seen normally well-balanced mothers besides themselves with frustration and anger at the fact that their child continues to wet the bed some years after bladder control is normally gained. The smell, mess and inconvenience really get to them and they became convinced that the child is doing it on purpose. But Joan, having once broken free from the apathy that had confined her to a wretched existence, was more than capable of dealing with a relatively minor obstacle.

How about the couple who cannot claim to have either acute nor chronic marital crises with which to contend, but who — while not desperately unhappy — could not claim to be happy either? There are thousands of couples like this, and they generally stay together either until a major crisis *does* occur or until they come across someone whom they very much prefer.

Sheila's and Bentley's was an example of a mediocre marriage which exploded suddenly into separation and divorce. They were a middle-aged couple; Sheila worked as an auxiliary nurse on permanent night shift in an Old Peoples' Home, while Bentley, appropriately enough, owned a garage where he repaired cars and sold petrol and a few groceries. Neither of the two came for counselling in the early days, but I saw them both from time to time for renewed prescriptions, since Sheila suffered from high blood pressure and Bentley was a diabetic.

Whenever they came to the surgery (which was always singly, never together), they would indulge in a good old moan about life in general and the institution of marriage in particular.

In fact, they always took up so much of my time that I used to ask the receptionist to give them a double appointment whenever they 'phoned up to see me. They were, they considered, incompatible — in rather a slow and undramatic kind of way. Sheila, for example, liked certain forms of love making, while Bentley was not at all interested in indulging her wishes in this respect. Sheila would have liked to become a vegetarian, while Bentley insisted on fried bacon for breakfast every single morning (which, of course, was rather inconsiderate of him, as this meant Sheila having to get out the frying pan and bacon as soon as she arrived home after a night on duty).

The very fact that their working hours were so different from choice, indicated how little they really wanted to share their lives. I asked Sheila one day why the two of them did not split up since she was always moaning about her husband. (I did not, of course, mention that Bentley invariably moaned just as much about her, as she did him, whenever he came to see me!)

'I couldn't possibly do that, doctor,' she protested, looking shocked. 'After all, we've been together for nearly twenty-six years now — and I can't imagine what the children would say!'

The extent to which the opinion of her adult children really mattered was illustrated six months after this conversation when a new male nurse was taken on at the Old Peoples' Home, and she fell in love with him! Thoughts of the binding power of twenty-six years, plus possible filial ridicule, had no deterrent effect whatever upon Sheila's determination to seek a divorce from Bentley and marry Marius at the earliest opportunity, once the two of them decided that their love was a permanent thing in their lives.

She came to see me when she had decided to go ahead with a new marriage — and again when she had been married for a year to her new husband. I had to congratulate her on how well she looked (she had ceased to come for blood pressure checks, soon after meeting Marius, for she went on a highly successful diet and lost sufficient weight to reduce her blood pressure to normal). 'Thanks, doctor, I feel marvellous,' she agreed. 'Marius and I are blissfully happy, and although I sometimes feel a bit guilty about leaving Bentley, I realize now that we only stayed together out of habit. There was very little true feeling between us — and certainly not the slightest bit of excitement.'

One other case history comes to mind, equally illustrative in its way. Dawn and Malcolm, engaged and in their mid-thirties, came to ask for help. They were troubled by Malcolm's impotence, for although he could get an erection from time to time, it was never sufficiently strong to enable him to make love to Dawn. I recommended them to the Clinic, after assuring them that the trouble was more than likely due to the stresses of divorce and change of lifestyle. Malcolm was in the process of being divorced by his wife on the grounds of infidelity and 'unreasonable behaviour', which he assured me were unfounded. Dawn had never, in fact, been married, but had a teenage mongol son who lived in a special 'home' and came home for most weekends.

I saw Malcolm about three months later when he had 'flu and asked him how things were going. 'They aren't, doctor,' he replied, with a wry smile.

> Dawn and I simply were not right for each other. To be quite frank with you, I resented every weekend being taken up by her son. Normally I don't think this would have bothered me, but I am under such strain at work at the moment, and what with worrying about the divorce and my sex problem . . . Yes, that began to improve, but we only went seven times in all. I was a bit upset when Dawn and I decided to call it a day, but I've no interest whatever in sex or women's company or anything at all, for that matter. I just feel so terribly tired all the time.

Divorce was clearly taking its toll so I gave him some general dietary and exercise advice, and left it at that. I knew that sexual problems were the last thing on Malcolm's mind at the time that we spoke, and was pretty certain things would right themselves once the divorce was out of the way and he had come through the 'divorce aftermath' phase successfully.

This, in fact, was the way things turned out for him — but the story had an unusual twist to it. He was obviously full of the joys of spring about a year later when he called into the surgery to have his ears syringed. He had found a permanent live-in partner, who was in fact the same sex as himself.

'It may sound funny, doctor,' he said, 'but I can honestly say that I've never felt happier nor more fulfilled in my life. My ex-wife was quite right really to accuse me of "unreasonable behaviour" — I've been buying gay magazines for years, and then she discovered that I am a transvestite too. I met John through a private gay dating agency and I would say they picked just the right partner for me. We are as happy as could be, together!'

I could not resist asking him about his sex problem. 'No trouble in that department either, doctor,' he assured me. 'I used to think that I was bisexual, being married but always secretly hankering after a male lover. Now I know the truth — I am attracted to men, and men alone; I wish I'd had the courage of my inner convictions when I left school and had started then to live the way of life I do now.

'I was just too scared of being laughed at.'

In the next chapter we shall discover how to decide between separation and divorce; the need to be perfectly certain about your choice; and how to put things into motion once you have decided definitely that your marriage should be brought to an end.

6.

SEPARATION OR DIVORCE?

In previous chapters, I have suggested circumstances, such as repeated physical assault and calculated mental cruelty, in which in the capacity of a doctor and a counsellor I would invariably advise the injured party to leave his or her partner without one moment's hesitation. Physical injuries can be fatal; and mental trauma just as fatal in a different sense, for the mind — our most precious possession — can be sufficiently badly damaged for complete recovery to be impossible.

I have seen men and women from all walks of life, from the simplest manual worker on the one hand to famous, talented professionals on the other — crumble intellectually and emotionally as a result of the mental torture inflicted by their marital partners. And one patient die from internal haemorrhage after her husband, home late and drunk as usual, beat her up once too often with a thick strap while she was still recovering from giving birth to his child.

However, even in the face of horror stories such as these, people continue to marry, make a good job of it, and achieve lasting happiness. What motivates others to remain locked in a relationship that is clearly going to destroy them, is often difficult to comprehend. But — as I made a point of stressing earlier — *only* those with intimate knowledge of a couple can form a detailed picture of the complex interaction between their two personalities. And only the man and woman concerned are really in a position to decide whether their life together is worth preserving.

The best a counsellor such as myself can do is to assess a situation in the light of normal human behavioural standards and whatever knowledge he or she may have of the two individuals concerned, and advise accordingly. If your devotion to your husband or wife is such that you are prepared to put up with alcoholism, physical assault, gambling debts or a home that is barely fit to house pigs, that is entirely your concern. Just make certain that you are there from choice, and not because you do not know how to go about extricating yourself from an intolerable marriage. And only possession of the facts of separation and divorce can enable you to make that choice.

Let us suppose that your marriage has recently been showing signs of wear and tear, and that you have just discovered that your partner has been carrying on with a colleague at work for the past six months. There is a dreadful scene when you tell him or her that you have found out about the affair, and since no apology, protestation of love for you or promise to terminate the relationship is forthcoming, you leave your partner while feeling shocked and betrayed — shouting before you slam the front door that you will be suing for divorce.

After a day or two when you have calmed down a bit, and had the opportunity to pour out your anger and grief to a friend or counsellor, you feel that possibly all is not lost and that you could conceivably be persuaded to 'try again' — provided your partner was equally willing. The best thing to do, is to telephone or write a brief note to this effect, suggesting that you meet on neutral territory to talk things over. Ask a close friend if you can use her lounge for your discussion, or agree to meet your spouse in a pub/park/restaurant — providing, of course, neither of you is likely to yell, scream or throw things if the discussion gets too heated.

Neutral territory is a good idea, for you are both more likely to make slightly more effort to behave reasonably if there is a chance of being overheard. The home environment may by its very familiarity, bring on feelings too difficult to control when your aim is an objective, rational discussion.

If he or she asks for 'a little more time' to sort themselves out, you'd be wise to agree. It is indisputably difficult to break off an affair while you are still in love — although you may well be aware that you are placing your marriage at serious risk by prolonging the relationship. So call upon the strength of your love for your husband or wife and work out a mutually acceptable length of time for him or her to sort out their feelings.

Make quite certain, though, that this separation is for a definite period of time and not an indeterminate one. Otherwise you may find yourself waiting month after month for the sorting-out process to take place — while you are being kept in intolerable suspense. Fixing the separation period at a month, two months, whatever, means that your partner is obliged to come to a decision, and hopefully to break off his or her affair with reasonable alacrity. And if the end of the agreed time is reached, without the vital decision having been made, then it's up to you whether you agree to an extension of the separation or decide straightaway on divorce proceedings.

Do not be inveigled into agreeing to extension after extension of the 'sorting out' period, or your partner may carry on indefinitely, neither ending the affair nor agreeing to divorce — while you are stuck out on a domestic and emotional limb awaiting a decision. And do not — whatever you do — agree to return home while he or she is deciding what course to take. Living elsewhere with friend or family achieves three things that returning home would never accomplish.

First, your departure and your projected return fixes the agreed length of the separation in the minds of both of you; it is far harder to insist that he or she comes to a decision within a specific time interval, if that period is interrupted by your early return. Second, you will both be under a strain, and bickering and rows are almost inevitable — which may make him or her opt for the new relationship and regret that decision later on.

Third, if you are the wife, your partner will be obliged to fend for himself during your absence, and if he is selfish and lazy by nature may well appreciate you far more if you do come together again. In any case, why should you keep house for

— or even with — him, and provide meals, clean clothes and a pleasant environment while he is off seeing his mistress and trying to decide whether to break it off with her?

There is a further advantage in a separation from your own point of view. If the two of you *do* decide to divorce, then living without your loved one for an agreed spell will have provided a relatively gentle introduction to a new way of life. And, however distressed you may be if you decide to go your separate ways, at least having lived without him for a month or two will be proof positive that you *can* survive on your own.

If the ball, so to speak, is in the other court, and *you* are the immediate cause of the rift by having a lover from whom you are trying to decide whether or not to part, try to get your husband or wife to agree to the arrangement I have just discussed. Be as gentle, but as firm as you can, trying to remember when abuse or domestic objects are hurled at you that you are inflicting a great deal of mental pain — and would probably behave in a similar way in a similar situation.

Ask for a separation of agreed length, determine to stick to it and reach a decision as soon as you can — and be as honourable as you would expect your partner to be in the same circumstances; and by this I mean *do not* move in for the agreed period with your lover or mistress, for this makes an objective assessment of the situation impossible. And *do not* invite him or her to move in with you. This makes objective decision making even more impossible, and is as insulting to your marriage partner as it is cruel to your lover — should you opt for ending your affair.

Just make absolutely certain that, whatever your decision, you will be able to stick to it permanently and without regret. Once the wheels of the divorce machine have been set in motion, the fabric of marriage is ground to particles of the finest dust and scattered remorselessly to the four winds. Be in deadly earnest before even making the first move towards this end.

Should you find yourself being sued for — or asked to agree to — a divorce, yet have no intention of forming a permanent relationship with anyone else, and had never wanted a divorce in the first place, then you will have to decide whether you should oppose the suit or let it go through without putting up any resistance. Some people are most anxious to preserve their image in the eyes of friends, relations and colleagues, and be the suitor rather than the sued party in event of divorce, so would be inclined either to countersue or to oppose the divorce suit being filed against them.

If you feel strongly about such an issue then you would have to decide on your reaction accordingly. My opinion is that the preservation of such an image may possibly be of value to someone who is prominent in society and constantly in the public's eye. For the rest of us, it hardly seems worth the bother to preserve an image about which the rest of the world really does not care a fig. To countersue, or to oppose a request for divorce on terms of mutual agreement, involves the expenditure of a great deal of money, time and emotional energy — which could be spent to far greater profit on yourself and your children after the divorce has gone through.

There is no point, either, however deeply hurt you feel, in trying to hang on to a partner who is bent on divorce. You can insist on him or her thinking things over for a bit before you are prepared to agree to divorce, in the hopes that his or her decision to end your marriage was a hasty one. But if you know in your heart of hearts that they are not going to change their mind, then agree to get the unpleasant business out of the way as soon as possible.

Let us return to the imaginary situation I outlined at the beginning of this chapter, one in which your husband or wife has decided to terminate his or her relationship with you and marry somebody else. And you have decided to sue your partner for divorce. What do you do first?

First, summon up your courage and find the best divorce solicitor you can. The names, addresses and telephone numbers of local solicitors can be found in Yellow Pages, and if you go to your local library and ask to see the Law List, you will find an entry for every solicitor in the country in much the same way that details of all Registered Medical Practitioners are available from the Medical Register, published annually. You will learn the essential details of any solicitor you may have heard of, including his degrees and the name of the university which bestowed them.

More important from your point of view, however, is whether you would rather employ a woman or a man as your solicitor and, having decided that, how to determine which firm and which individual to select. Solicitors, like doctors, specialize in a particular field, so find out before you make an appointment to see one, whether he or she deals with divorce. A conveyancing solicitor, for instance, however skilled he may be in preparing property contracts and conducting property searches, would not be prepared to manage the legal side of your divorce — so make sure that you will be dealing with the right person.

So far as finding a *good* one is concerned, many people maintain that this is very much the luck of the draw, and an even more precarious business than finding a pleasant Bank Manager or competent GP. But this need not be so, and as you cannot conduct a series of lightening interviews with half a dozen solicitors in order to pick the one who appeals to you the most — employ the next most satisfactory method and go by recommendation.

The chances are, of course, that although you may know several divorcees, not one is available for comment at the precise moment that you require the benefit of their opinion. The relative values of divorce solicitors are more than likely a closed book to you, since you have doubtless never considered that you would ever need to employ one. Resist the temptation, though, to ring round all the solicitors listed in Yellow Pages and make an appointment to see the first one who specializes in divorce.

Ask advice from people who know *you* — and the kind of person with whom you are happy to deal. Your Bank Manager may be able to help, and so may your doctor, dentist or Club Manager — all of whom mix socially with one another and with members of the legal profession. Ask friends, too, who though not divorced may well have other friends who are — and who can possibly recommend a divorce solicitor.

Just avoid the mistake I made, which was getting into a panic and utilizing the services of the first one I could find; he, unfortunately, took the standard phrase 'to instruct one's solicitor' quite literally, and 'phoned me for advice at every available opportunity, while proffering none himself. Uncertain of my rights, I ended up with a very poor deal.

If you want to know all you need to know about the legal

side of divorce, then consult a solicitor specializing in this field or, better still, buy a readable book on the subject and *then* make your appointment to see him. A good solicitor will, of course, be able to tell you all you need to know — but unless you take notes while you are with him (which, incidentally, is an excellent idea, as is a small portable cassette recorder providing he does not object to your using it) — you will need some information to which to refer between visits to him.

I would like to explain here why I suggested that you decide beforehand whether you would prefer to deal with a man or woman solicitor. You will probably be seeing, and speaking to, whomever you select as your legal adviser quite frequently during the months leading up to the Decrees Nisi and Absolute. You may be in an emotional state, overanxious, depressed and frequently tearful. So it simply makes sense to choose as your legal representative, the kind of person to whom you normally relate most easily when discussing personal matters. On the whole, men seem to prefer male solicitors but often opt for lady doctors, while women prefer on the whole to see a member of their own sex in either capacity.

Here, then, are some elementary facts about the way divorce proceedings operate. Since the change in the recognized grounds for divorce which occurred in 1971 (due in part to tireless campaigning by the Labour MP Leo Abse), divorce can now be granted in Britain when there is evidence that a marriage has broken down irretrievably. In practice, divorce is easier to obtain and in some respects more civilized, for at one time proven infidelity was pretty well the only ground on which it could be granted — and couples who were simply incompatible, were obliged to submit evidence of infidelity in order to gain their release.

Since it often happened that neither partner had been unfaithful, a great deal of trumped-up evidence had to be produced, with either husband or wife agreeing to spend the night — presumably, platonically — with a friend of the opposite sex who was prepared to be cited as co-respondent. There was a decidedly unsavoury side to divorce under those terms, too, for in order to be certain of obtaining a divorce from an unfaithful marital partner (who may not, in fact, have had any wish for a divorce) then evidence had to be obtained by subterfuge. Hence the employment of private detectives equipped with cameras, a manner sufficiently plausible to gain their entry into clandestine retreats, and sufficient patience and stoicism to see them through hours of waiting around in the cold and wet.

Since 1971, divorce is still granted in Britain for proven infidelity, and additionally after a continuous two year separation period when 'mutual consent' exists, i.e., if both parties are willing to terminate their marriage. A marriage is also deemed to have broken down irretrievably when the couple have been separated for a period of five continuous years and only one of them wishes a divorce to take place.

With respect to the Decree Nisi and the Decree Absolute, the former is granted before the latter and is a sign that unless some extraordinary obstacle occurs, the divorce is going through satisfactorily. It is appropriately named, since *nisi* means 'unless' in Latin.

The granting of the Decree Absolute signals that the procedure is complete, and that both parties are released from their marriage contract — and at liberty to remarry. It is difficult to say exactly how long a time elapses between the two Decrees — in my case the waiting period was about nine weeks. It is unlikely to exceed three months, but it does depend upon how the particular court concerned operates, and of course upon how busy they are.

Among the other aspects of divorce which may concern you are questions of property and maintenance; the custody of children; consent orders; and numerous other factors such as gaining access to the previous marital home, necessary changes in your Will etc.

As I have emphasized, I am no legal expert and would refer you to your solicitor or a book on the subject. But in case you are completely new to the subject, I will pass on the benefit of my limited knowledge. I should also point out that individual cases differ a great deal from one another as every couple's circumstances and requirements are peculiar to them.

Property and maintenance: generally speaking, unless the divorcing couple come to some other agreement, the marital home has to be sold and the proceeds subdivided between the two parties. If the couple are childless, the probable outcome will be equal division; if there are children, the parent who gains custody often is granted a larger share. Division of mutual possessions within the home is far better agreed upon by the two parties if possible. Otherwise a lengthy wrangle can develop over who is to get the washing machine, who the dining-room suite etc.

The law has also recently been revised in Britain on the vexed topic of maintenance — in favour, mainly, of the husband, who no longer has to face an inevitable future of monthly maintenance payments. A number of factors influence the outcome of a particular case, including the age of the couple; whether the wife earns money and how much; and her state of health. Also taken into consideration are the relative sizes of wife's and husband's annual income, and who is to care for the children and therefore spend most money on them etc. It seems fair, as the law now stands, that a husband should continue to support his children. But unfair — all things being equal — that he should have to pay his wife maintenance for the rest of their lives, if she does not remarry.

It is this latter state of imbalance that the revised laws seek to redress.

Custody of children: this is still more usually granted to the mother, but the father can contest for custody and may succeed if in the view of the Court he is a fitter parent than his wife to look after the welfare of the children.

Legal access: this normally refers to the granting of an access order to the parent not granted custody, in order that he or she may continue to see the children at certain agreed intervals. A parent granted unreasonably little access may appeal against the Court's decision in an attempt to gain more liberal terms.

Access to the erstwhile marital home may have to be negotiated between the solicitors for the two parties, during the interval between the divorce being petitioned for, and the sale of the home. This only becomes necessary when there is sufficiently bad feeling between the two parties for the partner still residing in the home to resist his or her spouse's entry by, for instance, changing the locks, buying a ferocious guard dog, or other comparable tactics.

7.

WHAT ABOUT THE CHILDREN?

The subject of children is brought up very frequently when marriage and divorce are discussed. The vast majority of couples do of course have children, but at least with the growing divorce rate, there is an increasing tendency to question the inevitability of children as part and parcel of contented married life. Some people cannot envisage life without several children, and would never feel fulfilled if they were lacking. More and more couples, on the other hand, are deciding that it is well worth suffering the oblique comments and questions of friends and relations, and opt for childless marriage — a decision at which they arrive for a variety of reasons. First — they may not actually *like* children! Which is, of course, an excellent reason for avoiding starting a family.

Second, they may feel they do not require children in order to be satisfied with life. This is especially likely to be the case when each partner has a stimulating and demanding job, which fulfils the creative urge — and a highly rewarding relationship with his or her spouse.

Whether to have children or not does not matter in the least, provided that each partner is equally happy about the decision and has the maturity to realize that his or her partner's attitude may well alter with the passage of time. When both partners start married life with the mutual decision *not* to have offspring, and later one or other of the couple starts to feel differently about it, marital problems can arise.

Some problems can be overcome with planning and forethought, as we have seen, but this eventuality is difficult to guard against, the best advice being the fullest possible airing of views on every aspect of the topic before marriage. One couple who came to me for marriage counselling, Pat and Eirlys, were on the point of separation. I saw them separately, and Pat told me that he felt that Eirlys was betraying him by suddenly wanting a baby:

> We've been everything to one another ever since the day we married. That was ten years ago, come March. Now that Eirlys is thirty, she suddenly wants a child. Aren't I sufficient for her any more? In any case, from what I remember of younger brothers and sisters, babies are noisy, smelly and demanding; and Eirlys, self-employed as an author and journalist, would never be able to cope!
>
> But will she see reason? Don't you believe it! Ever since she wrote an article on childbirth for a child-care magazine, and she started to take the magazine monthly, she has got more and more engrossed in the subject. *I* insist on continuing to use a condom — and consequently she has gone off love-making altogether!

I suppressed a smile, for Pat was really behaving pretty much like a small child himself when deserted by Mummy. I told him casually that he should be pleased, as I was certain that Eirlys wanted his baby because she was so much in love with him, not because he no longer satisfied her. And that this was — if he cared to think about it — a great compliment!

It is not always easy to help couples quarrelling over the children question, but fortunately Pat thought over what I said and must have decided that it could possibly be true. (I knew it was, for Eirlys had admitted as much to me!) Pat finally agreed with as good a grace as he could muster — and when their baby son was born exactly ten months later to the day, there was no prouder father visiting the Maternity Ward twice daily than Pat Owen!

The one time I would strongly advise against having children is when a marriage is failing, and starting a family represents to one or both parties a desperate attempt to cement the fragmenting edifice together. Children do not, in fact, make very good cement, and few marriages are actually saved from destruction by the arrival of a baby.

This is not to deny the hundreds of thousands of marriages whose continuing existence is solely due to the presence of children. But I would never recommend a couple to remain married to each other if they were each secretly longing for the youngest child to leave school — at which point they could up and go. Security for a child is as much a matter of an emotionally happy environment as it is one protected financially by two working parents. And when two adults dislike one another the atmosphere must often reverberate with antagonism and resentment.

I believe it is far better — and far more courageous an act — to admit that a thoroughly unsuitable marriage *is* just that, and to agree to separate and divorce while both partners are still young enough to enjoy life again, and possibly find another, more compatible, mate.

The next problem to clarify is the extent to which divorce affects children, and how any suffering on their part can be minimized.

So, how much *do* children suffer when their parents divorce? In the same way that there is no answer to the question: how long is a piece of string? There is no satisfactory reply to this imponderable query, other than to say that some suffer very much indeed, and others barely at all.

There are many factors influencing this important issue, and among these are: the age of the children, their relationship with both of their parents, the state of the atmosphere in the home prior to the break-up, and the arrangements made about their continued contact with the parent of whom they will see less than before.

Many parents claim that the older child suffers more than, say, a five-year-old; others maintain that the very young child is often more badly affected than his older brothers and sisters. Supporters of the main bulk of Sigmund Freud's teachings, on the other hand, state categorically that, while separation from either parent is likely to produce a degree of psychological damage regardless of the age at which it occurs, deprivation of either mother or father at the peak of any one of the three major developmental phases is equally destructive.

Essentially I adhere to the basic premises of the Freudian school of psychology and can appreciate how, for instance, losing Mother at the critical period of oral development sometimes can lead to depressive illness or schizoid tendencies in later life. But I firmly maintain that, if the situation is sensitively handled, children of any age profit rather than lose in the long run, by being removed from a household from which love between parents has disappeared.

An indispensable part of the proceedings is to explain to any child who is old enough to understand, exactly what has happened, and what is going to hapen, going to great lengths to point out that he or she is in no possible way to blame for the forthcoming family split. It is amazing, unless you have talked to a number of small children exhibiting signs of disturbance, how many of them blame themselves for the fact that Mummy is leaving Daddy, or vice versa.

It is also essential to reassure them that they will be seeing the departing parent at regular intervals, provided of course this is so. If you are having the children to live with you — and entertain the faintest suspicion that your ex-partner will let the children down — then try to be as reassuring as you can in general terms without making any promises. From the child's point of view, it is bad enough to be 'losing' Mummy or Daddy, about which he or she may well feel either guilty or hurt, or both, without having these harmful feelings compounded during the vital readjustment period by the non-materializing of promises.

So thrash out the whole approach you should adopt with your partner beforehand. And however desperately unhappy and bitter you may feel yourself, make an enormous effort not to let this spill out into your relationship with your child or children — especially if their existence (for which they are in no way responsible) contributed to the stresses that finally broke your marriage.

Children, on the whole, are extremely perceptive of their parents' feelings — and obviously you cannot sing, dance, smile and frolic when you are wondering how you are going to endure the misery of another single day or night. But show as much love as often as you can, and remember to provide, whenever possible, as many of the treats that were your husband's or wife's particular province. If you, as Dad, are assuming the role of single parent, do not forget to supply the bath-time games, the goodnight hugs or the tea-time treats which their mother used to give them. It is very difficult for small children to believe your assurances that they are loved, blameless and secure, if they are suddenly deprived of little things to which they have grown accustomed.

For the sakes of both you and the children, try to aim at a well-balanced and well-organized existence — perhaps even better organized than before the rift occurred. Slight haphazardness and a degree of unpredictability can be fun, but what children require more than anything straight after divorce enters your life, is a safe reassuring and stable environment.

So aim at set times for meals, bath and bed for the children, and if an acquaintance or stranger will be entering their life, do make sure to tell them about it first and arrange a meeting. It can be terrifying for a small child to cry in the night and be picked up by a strange baby-sitter whom you had forgotten to introduce.

By the same token, mention the existence of any new friends of the opposite sex whom the children have not met, and who may play any sort of a regular role in your life in the immediate future, even if no more than platonic. If you are divorcing, or being divorced, and intend to remarry as soon as the Decree Absolute is safely through, *make absolutely certain that your children get to know and hopefully to like your intended future spouse, before breaking the news to them that they are to have a new Mummy or Daddy.*

Children who are old enough to pick up nuances of an adult relationship long before you would have considered this possible, have a weapon to hand capable of inflicting considerable pain and embarrassment, so prepare for the possibility of this before introducing your new partner, especially if you half-expect a particular child to react with resentment. And try to strike a happy medium between showing a lot of love on the one hand, and refusing to put up with juvenile tyranny on the other.

For this very reason, I would avoid using the name 'Mummy' or 'Daddy' in connection with your new partner. Introduce your new friend/lover/mistress by their first name — and avoid the implication that he or she is about to take the place of the parent your child is missing. There is less likely to be rebellion, rudeness or tantrums, if your son or daughter does not feel that the image of the absent parent is being deliberately and heartlessly obliterated.

Sometimes your careful ploys work too well, and your children take so readily to their future step-parent that you fear that the next visit from their natural mother or father will be less than welcome. You may even feel that they prefer their 'new parent' to you! If this does seem to be the case, don't allow it to worry you! In the first place this is very unlikely to be true. Most children over-react, especially when their stability has recently received a severe jolt. And most of them know how to inflict a little pain on you — should they in fact blame the absence of their true mother or father on you.

Refuse to be perturbed by it, and the situation will soon rectify itself. Better, after all, this way round than that months of difficult readjustment should be needed for your future husband or wife to be accepted!

8.
THE AFTERMATH

Having spent some time considering the possible effects of your divorce on your children we should direct some attention to its possible effects on you. You may feel that this is not possible to predict; but just as there is a recognizable pattern to, say, the phases of grief following a bereavement, so enough people react in similar ways to the divorce situation for certain varieties of response to be forecast.

With respect to its ability to generate stress, divorce is ranked only one place down from the top of the list that evaluates the stress value of life changes as devised by Dr Thomas Holmes, Professor of Psychiatry at the University of Washington. Dr Holmes made a detailed study of the effects of certain types of stress upon physical and mental health and, as a result, evolved a Social Readjustment Rating Scale on which the higher values denote poor aptitude for readjustment to particular life changes than do the lower values.

Poor readjustment ability, of course, compounds stress and its deleterious effects upon our health and well-being.

The highest score was given to that most terrible of all personal tragedies, the death of one's spouse. This received one hundred points. Divorce was the next highest, at seventy-three. Other life changes whose values are of interest, were: marital separation (sixty-five); marital reconciliation (forty-five); pregnancy and sex difficulties (forty and thirty-nine respectively); and trouble with in-laws (twenty-nine).

The actual mechanism of divorce (let alone the effects of the initial breakdown) can produce a reaction of intense weariness. Early shock, if present (which it is in most cases, despite the fact that some couples discuss divorce for years before actually getting round to it), wears off gradually and is replaced by an intense urge 'to get the whole damned thing over with'.

So your immediate response to the granting of the Decrees Nisi and Absolute is likely to be one of profound thankfulness that the ordeal is finally over. Following the relief, and the accompanying slight diminishment of the stress factors, though, is what I always refer to as the 'aftermath' — and against which I try to warn all the patients who come to me for divorce counselling, including those who assure me that they will be delighted with their new-found freedom and liberty.

Having recovered temporarily from the shock of separation and having experienced some of the relief that the letters, telephone calls and legal consultations have now come to an end, most divorcees forget that they will have a tremendous amount of readjusting to do, with respect to lifestyle, financial income, the management of the children and even with respect to friends (some of whom fall easily into 'his and hers' categories, and others of whom are harder to place).

Characteristics of the 'aftermath' are: extreme weariness, physical and mental, accompanied by lethargy, poor powers of concentration, disinterest in normal pursuits and sometimes a recognizable degree of clinical depression. This is when the destructive thoughts that divorce engenders in most of its victims, come to the surface and have the greatest power to harm you.

You may suddenly start to feel acute emotional pain, that the initial shock of parting and the constant demand for action during the divorce proceedings period have not allowed time for. This may take you very much by surprise, just as you are congratulating yourself on your inner resilience and powers of swift recovery. Knowing about the possibility of this reaction, though, at least permits you to take some precautionary measures, and it should diminish its harmful effects to know that it, too, is a phase which, in common with fatigue, listlessness and general lack of interest, will disappear in time.

The emotional pain to which I am referring is likely to strike you in one of two ways. If you were the 'guilty' party in your divorce, then strong instincts of honest reappraisal, followed by the most terrible remorse, may bedevil your every waking hour. An insatiable desire to 'go back, undo the harm and start again', may dog you incessantly — and even half-persuade you that this would be possible, which of course it would not.

You may even start thinking that you must have been out of your mind to behave as you did, and feel tempted to seek your ex-partner with a view to effecting a reconciliation.

I am not for a moment saying that people have not managed successful reconciliations after divorce, which have lead to remarriage and happiness ever after. But this is not the usual course of events, its practical chances of success are extremely low — and *now*, while you are hyper-emotional and caught in the clutches of the 'aftermath', is the very last time on earth to consider such a possibility.

Someone once remarked — rather cattily, I thought — that my attitude was diametrically opposite that propounded in the Bible: 'what man has put asunder, let no God in Heaven ever try to reunite!' But an attempt at 'going back' at the parlous 'aftermath' phase is doomed to failure.

You do not get off very much more lightly if you were the 'innocent' party in the divorce proceedings, and agreed to a divorce only because you realized that there was no hope for the continued life of your marriage. As surprisingly easy as you may have found it to act reasonably, avoid major rows and violent reprisals for the sake of the children, and behave in an admirably civilized manner, an almost irresistible urge to 'get even' with your mate may well suddenly assail you.

So do not be too overcome with astonishment if plans for revenge infiltrate your every thought, and if you are subject to unusual outbursts of passionate anger, and tears.

Here is a little advice on how to avoid being lastingly damaged by your 'aftermath' phase and how you can bring the unpleasant reaction to an end as soon as possible, whichever form it takes.

First, allow yourself to cry, rant, rave and storm — either to yourself, in the new-found privacy of your new life, or in the presence of sympathetic company. This may even be your new mate, if you have one — for his or her presence is no guarantee against the onset of the 'aftermath' phase, and asking his or her help in the present acute crisis, is not the same thing as wearying him or her, day after day, with nostalgic recitals of your previous blissful marriage.

Also, as soon as you can manage the effort physically, do something active that actually tires you every single day. Smashing the hell out of a shuttlecock, tennis or squash ball, can help to relieve pent-up inner feelings of anger, resentment and hatred. And if you need some help in calming down after the session, do some yoga. You need not join a club if you do not feel like doing so — although, clearly, the sooner you get back happily into circulation, the better. If you are not ready for this yet, though, buy a book on the subject, wait until the children are at school or in bed so that you can be sure of minimal interruptions, and go through the simple stages of relaxation, correct breathing and muscular control. The benefits to your inner poise and shattered serenity, will be immense if you persist.

There is one important lesson to be learned from divorce, and that is the fact that neither innocence nor guilt is ever absolute. For, when a marriage breaks down due to physical assault on the wife, by a drunken pig of a husband, 99.99 per cent of the guilt can safely be placed on his hefty and brutal shoulders. But there always remains the odd 0.01 per cent which can be attributed to the wife.

It is very difficult to accept this fact sometimes, especially when the 'innocent party' is oneself. But it is impossible to state that any married person was ever wholly guiltless of provocation, unkind behaviour, or some degree of insensitivity, so try to grasp this straw of comfort if you are assailed by an intolerable burden of remorse.

If your problem is burning anger and resentment at the years you have wasted looking after and bearing the children of a brute who has left you for a sixteen-year-old redhead or, conversely, spoiling a selfish, ungrateful wife who has run away with your best friend, comfort yourself that you are wasting time no longer! You cannot reclaim the lost years — no-one can. But at least you are now free, and can make the very best of your life, choosing exactly how you wish to live it, and which objectives you should make your priorities.

If it is at all feasible, and you can afford it — treat yourself to a holiday in a spot you have always longed to visit, planning to start it about three months after your Decree Absolute is through. The stress of divorce must never be underestimated. You have been through a bad time, and consequently need a little pampering. Avoid going alone, though. The sight of all those happy couples playing on the beach with their children, walking arm-in-arm along the sea-front, or dancing to a romantic dinner band, will do nothing whatever to improve your present anti-social feelings, your loneliness or your battered self-confidence.

So persuade a friend to go along with you, giving him or her plenty of prior notice so that appropriate plans can be made. Or opt for a group holiday, which can be really good fun and is not as off-putting as it sounds. I, who have always detested the 'jolly old team spirit' — especially when it has been advertised as the essential ingredient in team games — decided to risk going on one, the year of my divorce.

The holiday I chose involved travelling to Morocco where a group of us fellow travellers met in Tangiers, then spent the following fortnight camping in the northern Sahara, visiting a number of out of the way native villages and spending the last day or so in magical Marrakesh.

It was the most exciting holiday I ever had, and there was such a wealth of new sights, smells, sounds and tastes to absorb, that there was not a single available moment to devote to self-pity. Nor for those powerful opposites, love and hate, to exert their damaging effects.

Love, you say? Exerts a bad effect on the person who feels it? The destructive potential of hatred does not need to be enlarged upon; but it should be explained that the enduring love for a lost object, can be very destructive indeed. Continuing to hanker after a relationship which is already in the past, or a loved one who has left you for someone he or she prefers, precludes enjoyment of the present — and of all the future has to offer. It can, moreover, make you old before your time, bitter and twisted in your approach to life, sexually impotent or frigid, and chronically sick into the bargain. These must, surely, be sufficient reasons for relinquishing this type of love — and possibly for seeking a replacement love-object with which or with whom to share your future?

Do not necessarily assume that a replacement *lover* is implied by this advice. You are at an extremely vulnerable stage when experiencing the 'divorce aftermath' reaction, having just lost some of your emotional and material security, and are busily engaged in recreating your strength, vitality and belief in life. The last thing you need at this time is another emotional involvement! Share some of your pleasure with others, certainly! But avoid any relationship that is in the very slightest bit likely to get serious.

Serious relationships necessarily demand that you give something of yourself in return for all that you receive. Such giving may be a joy and a pleasure. But the very action of 'giving' means a loss to some degree of a part of yourself. Wait at least until you are whole again, before you offer even a small part of yourself in a sexual/emotional sense. Sure, you get part of the other person in return. But who knows whether what he or she has to offer is exactly what you require right now to enable you to regain your health and strength? Why, therefore, risk depleting yourself further, before you are ready?

Other problems you may currently be facing, and which require all your reserves to cope with them, are: caring for your children alone (if you have custody); coming to terms with missing them (if you have not); coping with loneliness and freedom, and learning how to banish the first and make full use of the second; and steeling yourself to seeing or talking to your 'ex' from time to time, if this proves necessary.

You may, additionally, be trying to cope with paying the agreed monthly maintenance to your partner; or be trying to decide how on earth to manage, and whether to chase up your 'ex' in the event of such payments failing to materialize. We are going to look at how you can overcome some of these problems in the next chapter.

9.

YOUR NEW LIFE

Are you, as you read this, perhaps in the position of having recently divorced? And, having also gained custody of the children, could you perhaps be starting to wonder whether this victory was not a mixed blessing? It is not that you do not love them; nor that you would not have appealed against the Court's decision, had custody been granted to your ex-partner instead. But, as dear to you as they doubtless are, coping with children alone, after being in the habit of sharing the job, may well be taking all your reserves of love, patience and tolerance — not to mention money.

You may even be thinking that your partner got off scot free, while *you* are left — quite literally — minding the baby. For he or she has access to your offspring, and the pleasure of seeing them maybe once a week, while *you* have to put up with their moodiness and unsettled behaviour. There may also be hurtful comparisons drawn between your present daily lifestyle and the weekly excitement of a day in Mummy's/Daddy's new home — especially if Mummy or Daddy has recently acquired a new live-in lover.

Before you build up a store of resentment against them

remember that they, like you, are in the process of readjustment to a new lifestyle. If you cannot manage financially, contact your divorce solicitor again and see whether better terms can be agreed upon without the necessity of having to go to Court again. But if you are advised to take legal action, go ahead and do so. There is no room for squeamishness when money and maintenance are a big problem, and all the necessary contact can be carried out through your solicitors.

If the children are sometimes fractious, obstinate and critical, try to retain a sense of humour. Point out that you are very glad that they approve of your ex-partner's new friend; but that it is just possible that he or she could turn out to have an imperfection or two, were they the subject of constant scrutiny. And mention casually that you are far more interested in thinking of fun things to do together with them, than you are in hearing details of Mummy's or Daddy's new home.

This brings us to the vexed question of your contact with your 'ex'. If you have no children, then there should be no need for contact, and, while it *is* of course possible for a recently divorced couple to remain on amicable terms, this is a rarity, the majority of divorces furthering the gap that already separates unhappily married people rather than bringing them closer together.

Despite a whole world of excellent advice, only you, and you alone, can make sure that you survive divorce, and become happier and stronger as a result. And I certainly do not recommend continued contact with your ex-husband or wife as a good means to this end. One of your main objectives if you are to recover fully, is to learn to cease dwelling in the past. Agreeing to meet and talk to your ex-partner when this is not absolutely necessary, is a retrogressive step.

If you feel wretched or guilty at the mistakes *you* made during the course of your marriage, continued contact with the person concerned will only deepen this depressing state. If, on the other hand, you feel bitter and angry at the behaviour of your ex-partner, then you are unlikely to feel any better towards him or her just because you meet from time to time.

Whatever you do, avoid agreeing to future meetings (or trying to arrange them!) just because you feel lonely. You must expect to feel so sometimes, and with a little hindsight you can overcome this problem whatever age you are, and regardless of how little you may have mixed socially before your marriage ended. Little social contact, in fact, is often a feature of a strained marriage. Either you row so much and so often, you are not at all sure that the quarrelling would not break out in front of friends or — perhaps even worse — in public. Or you may simply be used to going your separate ways, which in the case of your particular marriage may have meant that your partner went out often — alone — while you remained at home, since there was nowhere you really wished to go.

Combat loneliness in simple ways at first, by noting when attacks of it are most likely to strike, and trying to find something to occupy you then. I counselled one patient to do this, and she told me that her loneliest period was just after arriving home in the evening from work, a time of day when she and her husband were accustomed to sitting and nattering about the day's events over a cup of coffee before getting the evening into motion.

She decided to get straight on to the sofa on arriving home, sleep for an hour, have a snack — then get started upon the daily study of a correspondence course she had always wanted to follow, in journalism and short story writing. Not only did this provide her with a new hobby, but she ceased altogether to feel depressed and 'out on a limb' when her first short story was accepted for publication.

Loneliness is only the other side of the coin, in fact, from freedom of action. Just as a miserable, pessimistic type of person will complain that his cup is half empty, while the happy and optimistic individual will feel grateful that *his* cup is half full — so you can regard having hours of your own company either as an insurmountable obstacle or as a new-found blessing.

Just think of the opportunities your new life affords. If you have children, you won't have much opportunity to suffer from real loneliness unless they are too young, or too busy, to be much company to you. If this is the case, invest in a reliable baby-sitter as often as you can afford to, and take yourself out somewhere. You may have colleagues at work, old school friends whom you have always meant to recontact, or a new friend or two who would be happy to go out in the evening or weekend with you sometimes. Otherwise, be brave and visit a cinema, theatre or art gallery alone — this can in fact often prove more rewarding than dragging along a companion who is not basically interested in the things that interest you.

If you do live alone, then plan your days just to suit yourself! Obviously this does not mean that you have to live selfishly, for you can if you choose, visit an elderly person, do some voluntary work in a hospital or just shop for an over-busy neighbour on a regular basis. But you have the marvellous opportunity so many of your married friends will genuinely envy, of using at least your leisure hours as you please without having to consult anybody.

You can spend Saturdays in bed, if you wish, listening to the radio and writing letters. You can go for a midnight drive deep into the country, without having to explain that no, you are not going to meet a lover, you simply enjoy driving along country lanes, through woods and over commons in the moonlight, while you play your favourite Mozart piano concerto on the car stereo.

You can, in a word, eat and drink what and when you like — or not at all, occasionally, if you don't feel inclined to. You can keep dogs, cats, white mice, a parrot — or even a horse, if you have the land — without interminable arguments being put forward against your idea. And you can be as tidy as you please, without discovering every few minutes that all your careful housework and neatness have been disrupted by a messy and inconsiderate partner.

This is a time for going to town — in every sense of the word, if the fancy takes you! You feel terribly lonely, sleeping in the double bed the two of you used to share? Sell the wretched object and invest in another, either a double one in which you can stretch and relax at will — without the distressing memories the old one brought back — or a new, comfortable single bed if you mean to keep your new-found independence (you can always swop it at a future date, for a new double, if you change your mind!).

Succumb to your loneliness, and you risk drowning in an ocean of misery and self-preoccupation. See 'loneliness' as the opportunity you need to develop your interests, personality and self-confidence, and you will thrive better than you would have imagined possible.

All the advice I have given — and give frequently to patients who ask for marriage and divorce counselling — is aimed at helping you to pick up the fragments of your life once your divorce is over, and to rebuild your future on a firmer foundation. It is compiled as a result of listening to, and observing, hundreds of men and women who are either facing marital problems or are trying to recover from the shattering effects of recent divorce. And partly, too, as a result of my own personal experience of both of these situations.

As you start to recover from the effects of the 'aftermath' stage, and to learn how to enjoy your own company, you will probably find yourself wondering what form your future will take, and whether you will always be single. Remember that you are only a passive toy with which Providence is free to play, as long as you are prepared to accept this role. If you wish to alter your life radically it is up to you to do so!

How do you feel, for instance, on the topic of remarriage? Your previous experience of marriage might have been so intolerable, or you may be enjoying your present, uncluttered existence so much, that the very idea is out of the question. On the other hand, you may secretly long to have another partner with whom to share everything — and feel that your life will never really be complete again until you have found a substitute for your first partner.

Before you rush out to join a singles' club, or write out a cheque to a computerized dating service, stop to consider whether this is *really* what you want of life in the long run. You may have got tired of going to places by yourself, and of feeling that you stick out like a sore thumb, at parties and dinner parties where all the rest of the guests seem to consist of married or courting couples. But before you settle definitely on finding another marital partner, ask yourself whether you really *need* another husband or wife?

You will have noticed that I castigated promiscuity earlier, as highly disruptive of a settled and happy married life. I certainly would not recommend it as desirable for even the confirmed bachelor or spinster. But there is a lot of difference between making endless one-night-stands a substitute for a permanent relationship, and indulging in the odd affair from time to time after you have divorced.

People who choose the former lifestyle, are often scared of the responsibility and the commitment that conventional marriage involves, or, for that matter, which a permanent and caring relationship outside marriage equally involves. But electing to have the occasional affair because you still need to give and receive sexual love yet have no wish to remarry can, if you are careful, be a wise idea.

It can also be a stupid and a selfish one, if you do not think very seriously about it beforehand. Certainly your need for a sexual outlet continues, regardless of the vagaries of human relationships, simply because it is one of man's primitive and instinctive functions. You may lose all interest in love-making, or suffer from a bout of impotence or frigidity when taxed on all sides by a collapsing marriage and the toils of divorce. But the feeling — and the need for fulfilment — will reassert themselves sure enough, once you are safely through the most stressful phases of your life change.

My basic message is: there is no need to get married, just because you can no longer do without sex. What you must avoid at all costs, is forming relationships with the wrong kind of people, and by this I mean anyone who falls into one or more than one, of the following groups.

First, vulnerable, sensitive and lonely people who may very much *want* to marry or remarry, and who consequently will be badly hurt if they fall in love with you and have an affair, only to discover that you haven't the slightest intention of marrying them. Second, anyone whom your instincts tell you, may attract you very deeply — and end by treating you in the same way. And third, anyone who so closely resembles your previous partner, temperamentally or physically, that the reason for your attraction has to be your subconscious desire to find his or her replica.

It goes without saying, too, that other people may pose a potential threat to your happiness and on those grounds should be avoided more carefully than the plague — for which, after all — there is now a cure! I am referring to individuals whom you may well meet before recovering properly from your 'aftermath', who impress you by their popularity, professional skill, success with the opposite sex or whatever, but who have some very undesirable habits which they may try to influence you to adopt.

These folk are not necessarily people with whom you might consider having an affair; they may well be members of your sex whose company you find exciting and stimulating, and for whom you rapidly form quite a powerful attachment. They may be charming, amusing, rich and successful — but they may also drink heavily; deal in drugs, which they also take; and have sex with all and sundry, notching up their victories with the sensitivity of a white slave trader.

My advice is, do not get involved at any cost! Individuals who live dangerously can whet your appetite for excitement and novelty, but the cost of becoming closely associated with them, can prove far higher than you would wish to pay.

Therefore, if your moral code permits, choose companions with whom you have something in common, and with whom you can share a number of interests; choose, above all, someone who not only possesses a sense of humour, but who has one compatible with your own. And, if you feel like it and they are agreeable and it *seems* right, share love-making with them too. But take great care, at the same time, *not* to contemplate marriage unless you are absolutely certain that it is the right decision to make. A second unhappy marriage, and a second divorce, are likely to take a far greater toll of your reserves than the first — however terrible an experience these may have been.

I promised to deal with every aspect of divorce from the emotional point of view, so feel that a few words of advice about remarriage should be included, since the very fact of divorce in a person's life greatly influences their attitude to future relationships — and even, for that matter, their ability to form these successfully. If they are unfortunate, for instance, they may form — and retain — a deeply cynical attitude to marital relationships, to the opposite sex, and even to life generally. So it goes without saying that advice is needed by many divorcees on the subject of future marital union.

Even if you have been lucky, have recovered from a bad marriage and divorce without undue trauma, and are seriously considering trying your luck in the marriage stakes for a second time, your whole approach to the subject is — or ought to be — vastly different from what it was when you were thinking of getting married first time round. You will be far more chary of making a mistake; deeply concerned that your children, if you have any, will take to a new partner; and most concerned that the two of you really do share the same ideas, objectives, interests and lifestyles.

Do not neglect the vital subject of sexual compatibility. Some people feel that, even when marrying for a second time, they should 'save themselves' for marriage, and avoid full intercourse before the wedding takes place. I do appreciate how they feel; but would not necessarily recommend it as good policy, especially if sexual incompatibility was a feature of the previous, unhappy marriage. Perhaps one of the wisest courses, in the long run, is to live together for six months or so while the possibility of marriage is in the offing, but before the two of you have definitely agreed to go ahead with it.

This is not a case of cynically 'trying and testing the goods', and returning them to the shelf in the event of their proving unsatisfactory. It is merely a wise measure to discover whether the pair of you are genuinely right for one another — or attracted, but not compatible, in the long term. Don't go too far in the other direction, however, and conclude that you are not sexually compatible if you experience some difficulty at first — either from frigidity or from impotence.

As we have seen, the most usual cause of sexual problems is a psychological one — and recent stresses and memories of sexual incompatibility with your previous partner, added to great anxiety that all should be marvellous in bed this time round, are more than enough to produce the very problems you are so at pains to avoid!

As I mentioned earlier, go and visit a marital Sexual Dysfunction Clinic together — you do not have to be actually married to attend. With love, patience and kindness, plus a refusal to panic, your problems should disappear without too much trouble. Explain the likely causes to your new partner, to put his or her mind at rest; and hope that he or she reacts with understanding and love. Overcoming this early problem together should have the effect of bringing the two of you even closer than before.

Tom and Jessie's case would be relevant to mention here. Both were patients in our practice and, although they did not know one another, both happened to join our panel of patients within a month of one another. Tom was a Company Director, married to a professional caterer who ran her own business, while Jessie was married to a well-known jazz musician. A couple of years after the two couples moved to the area, first Jessie, then Tom, came asking for marriage counselling.

Jessie's husband had gone to the States to play the cornet in a touring band — and had 'phoned at the end of the trip to say that he had fallen in love with a dancer, and would not be returning. Tom's wife, running an almost parallel course, had decided to leave Tom for a hotel manager with whom — as she told him before leaving — she had been having an affair for the past three months.

We saw the two of them through their respective divorces. Jessie's went through smoothly and in record time, Tom's turned into a horrible wrangle as his ex-wife strove for sole custody — she wished to emigrate with her new future husband who was returning shortly to New Zealand. Taking the children with her would, of course, be tantamount to denying Tom access.

While all this was going on, Tom and Jessie met at a dinner party and fell rather warily in love after dating one another for a month or so. They both came for counselling a number of times before agreeing that it would be right to go ahead and take the plunge. They decided to buy a house together and live with one another for a year, before actually deciding definitely on marriage.

This was when Tom's real trouble started, sexually speaking. He had not had intercourse for six months when he and Jessie first went to bed with one another and — in his own words — it was a 'disastrous failure'.

He couldn't even get an erection, let alone sustain one — and got so frustrated and upset that poor Jessie cried as well. So they came along together, wondering wherever they should turn for help. I mentioned the marital Sexual Dysfunction Clinic and — although Tom was not convinced that it could help him — he agreed to give the suggestion a try.

Therapy and counselling worked very well — and Jessie, too, started to enjoy sex a great deal more than she had before. Her husband Mike, had, it transpired, been her only lover, and had not been the best introduction to the art of love that a virgin could have. He had suffered from premature ejaculation, and took no trouble to stimulate Jessie — and she had never, once, experienced orgasm.

Tom's problems started to worry him less, from the time of his and Jessie's first visit to the Clinic. They ceased altogether as soon as the problem concerning his children and their whereabouts was solved, by a mutual agreement to have them with him and Jessie for three months every summer.

Tom and Jessie did eventually marry and were happy together — especially after their first child was born.

This brings us to the end of our consideration of the institution of marriage; of the factors most commonly responsible for its breakdown; of the attempts that can be made, to overcome marital problems; and of how — and when — divorce should seriously be contemplated. We have seen, too, how to go about getting a divorce, and how many people can expect to react, emotionally and physically, to the various phases of the proceedings.

I hope that I have succeeded in what I set out to do — which was remove the fear that many people feel for divorce and all it entails, and to assure them that if they are unhappily married a number of simple solutions are open to them. First, that they can seek to overcome whatever problems they and their partner may have by obtaining advice from a number of sources. Second, that if termination of the marriage is the only answer, then this is comparatively easy to bring about — and can be effected without terrible trauma to either party, if approached in the right manner.

And finally, that despite the deep emotional upset and stress that a major alteration of lifestyle can bring, you can safely expect to recover from the ordeal — *and* expect your life to be both a great deal happier and more satisfying.

USEFUL ADDRESSES

National Marriage Guidance Council
Herbert Gray College
Little Church Street
Rugby
Warwickshire

National Council for the Divorced and Separated
13 High Street
Little Shelford
Cambridge CB2 5ES

Gingerbread
35 Wellington Street
London WC2
(Organization run by and for one-parent families.)

INDEX

abuse, child, 72-4
advice
    sources of, 43-51
    unsolicited, 52-3
'aftermath' period, 95
alcohol dependence, 39-40, 60, 72
apathy, in marriage, 72-4

children
    after divorce, 100-101
    custody of, 86
    influence of, 75
church
    booked for wedding, 70
    ministers, 48-9
communal living, 12
cruelty
    mental, 35-7, 65-7
    physical, 35-7, 65-7, 72

Decree
    Absolute, 85
    Nisi, 85

divorce
    proceedings, 84-5
    reasons for, 21-42
    statistics in U.K., 21
drug dependence, 39-40, 60, 72

emotional pain, 95-6

friends (best), as counsellors, 51

hate, and love, 98
holiday, benefits of, 98
Holmes, Dr Thomas, 94
homosexuals, 13-15

illness
    mental, 25-8, 58-60
    physical, 25-8, 58-60
infidelity, 28-30, 60, 72
interests, divergent, 30-32, 61-2

legal access, 86-7
loneliness, 101-104

lovers
  affairs with, 60-61, 99
  and children, 93
  v. marital partners, 16-18

maintenance, 85-6
marriage
  alternatives to, 12-20
  benefits of, 11
  guidance counsellors, 45-6
  origins of, 9
ministers (see church)
money (and marriage), 58

parenthood, reluctant, 37-9, 67-9
parents
  as counsellors, 49-51
  of teenagers, 55-6
  returning home to, 55
past, morbid adherence to, 41-2, 69
physical exercise, 97
present, refusal to accept, 69
property, 85-6

reaction, to divorce, 95
redundancy and unemployment, 24-5, 56-8
Register Office, booked for wedding, 70
remarriage, 104-107

separation, 78-82
sexual
  dysfunction clinics, 46-8, 62-5, 107
  problems, 32-4, 62-5
social readjustment rating scale, 94-5
solicitors, how to find one, 82-4
stress, divorce and, 94-5

teenage marriage, 22-4, 53-6

working hours, as source of stress, 57-8

yoga, 97